This b
Lanc

THE
WORKERS'
WAR

THE WORKERS' WAR

BRITISH INDUSTRY
AND THE
FIRST WORLD WAR

ANTHONY BURTON

The
History
Press

Cover illustrations: *The Illustrated War Times* and *The Time History of War*

First published 2014

The History Press
The Mill, Brimscombe Port
Stroud, Gloucestershire, GL5 2QG
www.thehistorypress.co.uk

British Library Cataloguing in Publication Data.
A catalogue record for this book is available from the British Library.

ISBN 978 0 7524 9886 7

Typesetting and origination by The History Press
Printed in Great Britain

CONTENTS

INTRODUCTION

The inescapable visions of the First World War are of the slaughters in the fields of Flanders and the miseries of the trenches. It is a war that had been characterised as one of brave soldiers led by incompetent generals, or as it has often been more pithily put 'lions led by donkeys'. But this is only a part of the story: it was also a war of competing technologies. Had it been fought fifty years earlier Britain would have begun with huge advantages as the world's industrial superpower. This was the country that had created the Industrial Revolution and become the greatest manufacturing nation on earth. But warning notes were being sounded as early as 1838, when Benjamin Disraeli said, in a speech in Parliament, 'The Continent will not suffer England to be the workshop of the world'. He was right. In Derry and Williams' book *A Short History of Technology* (1961) – an interesting title for a volume with nearly 800 pages – there is an appendix listing important technological advances made throughout the world. During the period from 1760 to 1810, the conventional timescale adopted for the Industrial Revolution, forty-one important discoveries and inventions are listed for the United Kingdom, compared with only twenty-one for the whole of the rest of the world. Move forward to the second half of the nineteenth century and things look very different. Between 1850 and 1900, thirty-four inventions are recorded for Britain, compared with ninety for everyone else, with an increasingly large proportion coming from America. Britain was still a major industrial power when the war began in 1914, but it was no longer the greatest innovator. The country was suffering the fate of many who take what they see as an unassailable lead: they had slipped into complacency.

What was true of industry was no less true of the military. Britain had faced no real military threat in Europe since the defeat of Napoleon, so no one felt any urgent need to modernise either military technology or tactical thinking. If the leaders of industry had become complacent, they were positively revolutionary compared with the majority of generals and admirals. But the war that began in 1914 was going to require the country to change dramatically. Industry would have to be reorganised, develop new ideas and change its whole way of working to compete with the industrial might of their opponents. The military would need to adapt to a new sort of warfare of a type that had never been known before and that would use weapons that had scarcely been considered even two decades earlier. The country would also have to adapt to a situation it had not known for centuries. Britannia had ruled the waves for as long as anyone could remember but did so no longer, simply because a new enemy had appeared that the navy had not prepared itself to combat. The threat was no longer from mighty battleships firing broadsides, but from a secretive enemy lurking out of sight in the depths, the submarine. And if Britain no longer controlled the seas, then that would have a huge impact in a country that had come to depend for its prosperity and very life blood on international trade. This would be in every sense, a war unlike any other. It would be a war where what happened on the home front would be every bit as important as what happened on the battlefield.

The war years were not only a time of enforced, rapid technological change, but of great social change as well. The ruling ethos of laissez faire in which the government assumed that the best thing to do with industry was to leave it alone to sort out its own problems had to be abandoned. Confrontation between management and workers, with its inevitable succession of strikes and lockouts, had to give way to co-operation for the general good. With hundreds of thousands of men leaving all industries for the armed forces, someone had to fill the vacancies, and they were to be filled in many, many cases by women. There would be no shortage of sceptics who were convinced that the 'weaker sex' would be better off doing the sort of things they were 'supposed to do', and if they wanted to help the war effort they could always knit socks for the men on the front. The women who moved into factories, who worked on the buses, helped run the railways and drove trucks were to triumphantly prove the sceptics wrong. It was one of the great revelations of the war years that forced a reassessment of the roles of the sexes.

Superior technology can win wars. A small British force could trounce a mighty French army at Agincourt simply because they had the longbow and the French didn't. In the nineteenth century the Opium Wars were over in no time at all because Chinese junks were no match for British gunboats. The war of 1914–18 was different. Both sides started on a more or less even footing, but both sides had to develop brand new technologies at an unsurpassed rate. It was a question of who would make the big technological breakthrough first. To understand the problems facing the industrialists of Britain it has been necessary to look back a little in time: what happened in the war years makes little sense unless one has some idea of how the various industries had arrived at the state they were in when it started.

In this book I have tried to look at how the different industries coped with the demands of war, but it is not just about technological and political advances. I have also tried to show the heroic efforts made by the ordinary men and women of Britain to overcome hardships and their enormous efforts to keep industry moving forward. The men in the British trenches fought a terrible war against the German soldiers lined up against them across the blood-drenched wastes of no-man's-land. That they won was due in no small measure because of the other war being fought between the workers in the industrial regions of Britain and their opposite numbers in the Ruhr. This is the story of that war.

1

BUSINESS AS USUAL

When the Great War began in 1914, it was not intended that it should be a great war at all: it should have been a brisk affair, comfortably over in time for the troops to enjoy Christmas at home. Back in Britain, life would continue much as it had before: it would be 'business as usual'. We all know now that the high optimism of the first few months soon died in the horror of the trenches. Far from being business as usual, life in Britain was to change dramatically. A.J.P. Taylor at the start of his great history of Britain between 1914 and 1945 wrote that, 'Until August 1914 a sensible, law-abiding Englishman could pass through life and hardly notice the existence of the state, beyond the post office and the policeman.'¹ In the following four years, all that was to change dramatically and nowhere was this more keenly felt than in the world of industry. The government would take control of some industries, regulate pay, impose restrictions on what could and could not be produced. It would ration food and tell farmers what to grow. It would introduce a section of the population, which had been all but absent from many traditional industries, to a new way of life. For the first time, women would appear in the workforce in a whole range of occupations that had previously been considered uniquely suitable for men. Nothing would ever be quite as it was before. In this book we shall be looking at the industrial world of Britain during these four years, the immense changes that occurred and how those changes had a profound effect on the whole of the civilian population. But nothing that happened at home could be divorced from the way in which the war was fought on land and sea and in the air.

It is not unreasonable to say that in August 1914 those in charge of Britain's armed forces were anticipating waging a war that would be more or less like the wars of the past. On the battlefield, the artillery would exchange bombardments, infantry would advance and the cavalry would swoop down to finish things off. At sea, mighty warships would blast away at each other until one fleet was either crippled or turned tail and headed back to port. Britannia, it was assumed, would continue to rule the waves as it had throughout the nineteenth century. The idea that new technologies might have a decisive effect on the way the war was to be fought simply did not seem to enter anyone's mind: at least not into the minds of generals and admirals.

At the start of the war the basic assumption that little needed to be changed was borne out in practice: guns would be hauled on the battlefield just as they had been at Waterloo by teams of horses, and the most efficient way to send a message from one commander to another was to give it to a man on a horse. That is why every infantry division of 18,000 men was accompanied by 5,600 horses. Throughout the war, the army continued to rely on its four-legged transport: in 1917 there were around 600,000 horses and 200,000 mules on army work. Yet as early as 1769 a former officer from the Austro-Hungarian Army, Nicholas-Joseph Cugnot, had invented a steam tractor specifically designed for military use. It has to be said that it was not a huge success. It suffered from one serious drawback as far as use by the army was concerned: the boiler only held enough water for twenty minutes' use, after which it had to be allowed to cool down for another twenty minutes before it could be refilled. The idea of having an immovable target for the enemy for that length of time would have ruled it out for practical use. To add to that, there was a major problem with steering the cumbersome beast. According to a possibly apocryphal story, the problem was so acute that on its initial trial the machine got out of control and demolished a brick wall. At that point the authorities stepped in and arrested the inventor before he could do any more damage. It was to be nearly forty years before another steam carriage appeared on the scene, designed by the wayward Cornish engineer, Richard Trevithick. He overcame the steering problem by putting his engine on railed tracks, marking the start of the railway age.[2] Communications problems could have been largely solved by the use of an existing technology, the field telephone: the army did not have any. Everything in 1914 was geared up for a mobile war, not one to be fought between armies crouched in trenches that stretched from the English Channel to the Swiss border, emerging at intervals to be mown down by machine-gun fire in the vain hope of making some sort of decisive breakthrough.

The early developments in mechanical transport may not have been successful and when success did come in replacing the horse by a machine, it was purely for civil use. But it is still remarkable that no serious attempts were made to mechanise the army until the arrival of the internal combustion engine. Even then there was little enthusiasm for the idea.

The navy had been no more enthusiastic than the army to adapt to the new steam age. At first they saw the steamboat as a useful device for towing large sailing battleships out of harbour. By the start of the Great War, however, the steam fleet was well established and included fast vessels powered by the new turbine engines developed by Sir Charles Parsons. His experimental steam yacht *Turbinia* gave a dazzling show at the Spithead naval review of 1897 when it raced across the front of the assembled fleet at the previously undreamed of speed of 34 knots. It must have been an incredible sight, with the busy crew getting up as much steam as they could, so that flames and red-hot cinders shot out of the funnel, leaving the little craft with a fiery wake.[3] The turbine engine had proved its worth, but there was still the same sense that a war at sea would be fought in much the same way as Nelson had fought at Trafalgar, but with bigger guns. Shipbuilders had produced ironclads with heavy armament and good protection along the sides of the ship to withstand a broadside, but the German battleships fired from a greater distance on a higher trajectory. As a result, the shells fell like bombs on the less protected decks. This was easily remedied by adding extra armour plating, and the mighty British Navy was ready for a major battle with the German fleet. But the Germans declined to come out except on their own terms.

The Royal Navy was known to be spread all round the south and east coasts to protect against a possible invasion. On 15 December 1914 a formidable German battle fleet headed off for the north-east coast of England, led by two fast battle cruisers and a cruiser. The intention was to lure a small part of the dispersed British fleet into an engagement and inflict heavy losses before heading back quickly to home waters. The targets were scarcely of major military importance. The fleet divided, and the first barrage hit the seaside resort of Scarborough early on 16 December in a heavy bombardment that left fourteen civilians dead. The ships moved on to another undefended port up the coast, Whitby, where among the buildings that were damaged was the ancient Abbey of St Hilda high on the cliffs. Once again, civilians were the only casualties. In spite of German claims to the contrary, neither town possessed any form of coastal defence, nor did they contain a single site of military importance. The third attack by the other section of the German fleet took place at Hartlepool, which did at least have a military presence, and the battery there managed to land a shell on the German vessel SMS *Blücher*, inflicting some damage. The destruction here was much more severe and 102 died, including fifteen children. A cruiser and submarine in the harbour at Hartlepool were unable to leave port. British destroyers attempted to engage with the Germans and managed to fire off one torpedo, but mist came down and the battle was over.

The event caused shock and outrage throughout Britain. The press reported it as a cowardly action in which, once the British ships appeared, the Germans fled: 'The raiding ships were not allowed to bombard the coast with impunity. British patrol vessels promptly engaged them, and a patrolling squadron at once set off in the endeavour to cut them off. When they found themselves in jeopardy the enemy ships "retired at full speed".'[4] Posters were rapidly produced with appropriate messages

– 'Remember Scarborough – Enlist Now'; 'Men of Britain will you stand for this?' It added further fuel to the already almost hysterical war fever, but it also provided an omen for the future. For centuries Britain had fought wars in other people's countries. This one would also be fought at home. It helped to convince the people that this was a war in which everyone was involved, not one that was read about in the papers, fought by professionals in far off places.

After the skirmish off the north-east coast the battle fleets failed to meet in any major conflict until 1916 at the inconclusive Battle of Jutland, but in the meantime a very different war at sea was to have an immense impact on life in Britain. It was to be waged not by mighty, heavily armed capital ships, but by submarines. The British Admiralty was mostly contemptuous of the whole notion of submarine war-fare. In 1900 Rear Admiral A.K. Wilson famously declared that the submarine was 'underhand, unfair and damned unEnglish'. Admiral John 'Jacky' Fisher who watched submarine trials at Plymouth in 1904 took an entirely different view, declaring himself astonished that so few among his fellow officers understood just how significant this new development was. This view was expressed even more strongly by Admiral Percy Scott shortly before the outbreak of war in June 1914. He wrote to the leading newspapers[5] and began his letter with a quotation from the First Lord of the Admiralty, Winston Churchill: 'But the strength of navies cannot be reckoned only in dreadnoughts, and the day may come when it may not be reckoned in dreadnoughts at all.' Admiral Scott took the argument a step further, claiming that the day had already arrived: 'as the motor car has driven the horse from the road, so has the submarine driven the battleship from the sea'. For the next few days the correspondence column of *The Times* was full of naval experts pouring scorn on these ideas. The Secretary of the Navy League roundly declared that: 'No competent naval authority will hold that the submarine has reached that stage of evo-lution which would justify Sir Percy Scott's estimate of its fighting value.' He went on: 'His views are premature, ill-advised, and calcu-lated to do serious harm to the cause of the maintenance of British supremacy at sea.' *The Times* added its own view in an editorial:

'there is nothing, even in peace experience, to justify the faith he places in torpedo attacks'. One correspondent summed up the views of many – spending money on submarine development was a waste of resources: they were 'just marvellous toys'.

The submarine had a potentially powerful weapon, the self-propelled torpedo, first invented by Robert Whitehead in 1866. Early versions were more than a little wayward, but various improvements, including a balance chamber to maintain the missile at a fixed depth and the addition of a gyroscope to keep it in line, made it a formidable weapon by the early twentieth century. The Whitehead torpedo was matched by a German version, known as the Schwartzkopff: someone seems to have had a sense of humour as this translates as Blackhead. It was a powerful missile capable of carrying up to 200lb of TNT in its warhead. The British saw the torpedo as a weapon mainly to be deployed by specialist surface craft, especially fast destroyers. The submarine was merely an adjunct, a slow form of torpedo boat and not an effective weapon of war. The idea of using it against merchantmen was abhorrent and one admiral declared that sinking civilian ships was piracy and any crew involved should, if captured, be hung. It was assumed that the war would be carried out under 'cruiser rules'. Enemy merchantmen could be taken, but first a warning shot had to be fired, then the crew and any passengers had to be given time to get into lifeboats before any further action was taken. This made the submarine almost useless. Its one advantage was its invisibility under the waves: on the surface it was slow and made an easy target. Churchill had given his opinion that no 'civilised power' would sink merchant ships without warning. But as early as January 1914, Lord Fisher had sent him a memo explaining the real logic of the situation:

> [The submarine] cannot capture the merchant ship, she has no spare hands to put a prize crew on board, little or nothing would be gained by disabling her engines or propeller, she cannot convey her into harbour, and, in fact, it is impossible for the submarines to deal with commerce in the light of international law … there is nothing else the submarine can do except sink her capture.[6]

But if the British were writing it off as a marvellous toy, the Germans had other ideas. Experts may have scoffed at the threat, and dismissed the torpedo as too unreliable to be effective, but on 5 September 1914, the German submarine U-21 sank a British cruiser with a single torpedo. Only nine of the 268 crew survived. Three more British cruisers were sunk by the end of the month and panic spread through the Admiralty when a U-boat managed to penetrate the defences at Scapa Flow, where much of the British war fleet was at anchor. It was not able to do much damage, but it showed that this was a powerful new weapon of war. In the event, it was not attacks on other warships that were to prove important but attacks on merchant shipping.

Germany announced that any vessel from any country trading with Britain would be considered a target for attack. There would be no warnings: 'cruiser rules' no longer applied. The new tactics were ruthlessly applied, culminating in the sinking of the British passenger ship RMS *Lusitania* in May 1915. It went down in eighteen minutes with the loss of 1,198 lives, which included 128 American citizens. *The Times* unsurprisingly called it an act of barbarism, but in its editorial it pointed out a possible reaction to the tragedy. Beginning somewhat disingenuously, 'It is not up to us to speculate upon the course to be adopted by the United States Government', the editorial proceeded to offer some very strong hints that it was time for reprisals. After all, the US Government had sent an official note to Germany as recently as February that year stating firmly that they would take 'any steps neces-sary to safeguard American lives ... on the high seas'.[7] The response across the Atlantic was ambiguous. *The New York Times* headed its account, 'Divergent views of the sinking of the Lusitania'.[8] It was pointed out that Germany had warned everyone that it intended to make such attacks, and the *Lusitania* was a British vessel and therefore a legitimate target. Nevertheless, there was concern in Germany that the Americans might be provoked into joining the war if there were any similar attacks, which was the last thing that they wanted. There was a temporary easing of U-boat attacks, but it was only temporary.

Towards the latter part of the war the British found a partial answer to the submarine threat by sending merchantmen out in protected convoys, which if they did not prevent attacks, gave the British fleet a chance to attack the attackers. The Admiralty had been reluctant to use the convoy system, because they still thought of the navy's battleships as having been built to fight decisive battles with the enemy fleet. They were there for offence not defence: it was a view that had catastrophic consequences and threatened the whole war effort. The losses were colossal, totalling nearly 13 million gross tons of shipping, half of which was lost in just one year, 1917. The German U-boats suffered their own severe losses, roughly half of the 351-strong fleet was lost and some 5,000 submariners killed. But there could be no doubt of their effectiveness. Neutral ships were deterred from trading with Britain, and the British fleet was not, by itself, able to keep up with the demand for goods needed on the home front. In pre-war years the country had become more and more reliant on all kinds of imports, from foodstuffs to the raw materials of industry. When these were no longer available the country was forced to try and make do with what was available at home. It was a state of affairs that affected everyone from the industrialist to the housewife. The situation was so serious that for a time it seemed that Britain would be so starved of resources that the war could be lost. Huge efforts had to be made by all sections of the community to save the country from catastrophe.

The attacks from the sea in 1914 had awoken the British to the idea that their own country was now part of the war zone. The naval bombardment came as a considerable shock, but another threat would soon appear.

Ferdinand von Zeppelin spent his early life in the army and was keen to study modern warfare. As a young man, with nothing exciting happening in Europe, he managed to get himself to America where he joined the Army of the Potomac in the Civil War. In his own words: 'I believe it my duty to use this opportunity through travel to gain information that I may be able to use for my fatherland at some time.'[9] It seems extraordinary that there should be any connection between an event that seems as remote as the American Civil War and the Great War that still resonates with us today. Yet it is Zeppelin who provides the link. Returning to the peacetime army in Germany, he was fascinated by the implications of the balloon as an aid to reconnaissance in the field, but began speculating about how much more effective the balloon could be if it could be powered and steered. It was this that led him to develop an airship with a rigid frame. Initially it was developed for civil use and the Luftschiff [airship] Zeppelin 1 (LZ1) took to the skies in 1900. Over the next decade it was developed into a highly successful passenger-carrying craft, but as soon as war broke out Zeppelin's first three airships were commandeered for use by the army. They were soon adapted for carrying bombs instead of passengers and, on 17 March 1915, Zeppelin ZXII set off to bomb London. It was not a promising start. The crew found themselves in dense fog and, after cruising around for some time, they failed to locate the Thames estuary, so they turned back south and bombed Calais instead.

Zeppelin raids continued over the southern and eastern counties of Britain, but had very little effect in the sense of causing meaningful damage. In order to avoid being hit by ground fire – and with the body full of inflammable hydrogen they were highly vulnerable – they had to fly at well over 10,000ft. At this altitude, life for the crew was cold and uncomfortable, navigation difficult and the chances of hitting any designated target negligible. People became quite complacent and regarded the arrival of the slow-moving cylinders high above their heads as something of a sideshow:

> After a week in which there have been more than the usual number of air-raids on the 'Eastern Counties' and even on 'the London District' the British public may fairly congratulate themselves on the complete failure of these nightly visitors to achieve any moral or military success … the Zeppelins have offered an exciting spectacle to thousands of honest citizens, who show their indifference to the raiders when they appear by parading the streets of the Eastern counties and the London district in defiance of every rule and regulation.[10]

My mother was a young girl in Stockton-on-Tees during the war years, a town that, as a shipbuilding centre, was a likely target. She vividly remembered the slightly sinister long, grey shapes passing overhead and rushing out into the garden to get a better look. It was all very different from the next World War, when my grandmother, still living in that same house, was forced to spend many nights in the Anderson shelter in the front garden.

As the war progressed, the Zeppelin raids increasingly gave way to attacks by aircraft. The early attempts were no more successful by plane than they had been by airship. The Germans offered to award a medal to the first airman who managed to land a bomb on Dover. It was won by a gentleman called Traube, though his one and only hit landed in a kitchen garden. He received his medal and, thanks to his success, one Dover resident had a ruined greenhouse. It seems that the air raids were taken no more seriously than the Zeppelin raids had been. It was a contest between planes with no really successful means of aiming their bombs and anti-aircraft batteries that found it equally difficult to master the new problem of hitting an aeroplane. It appears to have been regarded almost as a spectator sport, with crowds turning out to cheer the gunners. The first attempt to down a plane over Dover turned out to be more farce than high drama:

> On May 3 at 10.55am, an aeroplane coming from France and thought to be hostile was fired on for nearly ten minutes by the Dover guns … It was the first time anti-aircraft guns had been in action in Dover, and created intense excitement in the town. People rushed on to the Sea Front and expressed the greatest disappointment at the shots failing to hit the target … It was fortunate, however, that it was not hit, as it happened to be one of our own machines.[11]

There were to be over 100 raids on Dover and, although thirteen men, one woman and three children were killed, there was no real damage done to the port. The air raids did, however, have a demoralising effect on everyone in the country. The government imposed blackout regulations and the streets were plunged into darkness every night.

There were many aspects of the war that would directly affect the way that life in Britain was lived during the war years, but none had a greater effect than the disappearance of so many men into the army. There was no industry, no occupation that was not affected to some degree or other. When war began there was a patriotic rush to arms. Men believed it would all be a great adventure, in which the splendid British forces would emerge triumphant as they had in previous European wars. Eager young men wanted their share of the action and their moment of glory before it was all over, as all the experts declared it would be, in just a few months time. It was soon all too clear that not only would it not be finished by Christmas, but that it would develop into a long war of attrition with ever mounting casualties, so that more and more men would have to be sent to France. As a result, vital industries found themselves with a serious manpower shortage and many posts that would once have been thought entirely unsuitable had to be filled by women. It represented a massive social change.

The need for another great change that would be brought by the war was not immediately recognised and in some cases never accepted. This was to be a war that would eventually be fought and decided, in part at least, by new developments in technology. The reluctance of the old guard to accept change was typified by attitudes among the army top brass. A.J.P. Taylor pointed out that, thanks to the British generals' unshaken but entirely mistaken belief that eventually cavalry would win the day, more shipping space was taken up sending animal fodder to France than was lost to submarine attacks.[12] But it was not to be horses that decided the issue. It could be argued that many of the decisive battles of the war took place not in France but in the factories of Britain and Germany. It is the story of that war that we shall now be telling.

2

RAILWAYS

The day the war started, all the railways in Great Britain came under government control through the Regulation of the Forces Act 1871: Irish railways remained independent until the beginning of January 1917. The government took over a far more extensive system than the rail network we have today, with over 20,000 miles of track split up between companies that ran the full gamut from the mighty Great Western empire, covering the whole of south-west England and most of southern Wales, to the 19-mile-long Lynton & Barnstaple Railway. It was also a very busy system. In 1912 statistics recorded 514 million tons of freight being carried and 1,265 million passenger journeys made, not counting season-ticket holders. To put those figures in perspective: the population at the time was 46 million, so that is equivalent to the entire population making an average of one train journey every fortnight, and can be compared with the 46 million journeys registered in Britain today, which means we now average rather less than one journey a year per person. It was also highly profitable with working receipts of £124 million.[1] Yet in 1914 company profits were no longer to be a priority: there was to be only one all-important concern, winning the war.

A new organisation had already been set up and was ready for action the day war broke out, with railway management passing at once to an executive committee, made up mainly of managers from the leading companies. They did their work well. One of their first tasks was to call a meeting with the leading trade unionists from the National Union of Railwaymen and the Associated Society of Locomotive Engineers and Firemen to ensure their full co-operation. The unions agreed to a truce. There would be no strikes over disputes about job allocation, and any disagreements over pay would be settled by government arbitration. One can be sure that the union officials did no more than represent the patriotism that had its effect on their workforce just as it did on the rest of the country, but it was also a big step forward in co-operation between management and workers. The unions were now formally recognised as representing the whole workforce and not just their own members. For the first time they also had a right to have their views taken into account on any changes in working practices. Theoretically, industrial action was officially ruled out for as long as the war lasted.

The results of the enthusiastic co-operation were rapidly apparent. The first necessity was to move men and equipment to Southampton for embarkation with the British Expeditionary Force. In the first month, 670 special troop trains were run and the Secretary of State for War, Lord Kitchener, expressed his delight in a speech in the House of Lords: 'The Railway Companies in the all-important matter of the transport facilities, have more than justified the complete confidence reposed in them by the War Office, all grades of the railway services having laboured with untiring energy and patience.'[2]

The new ruling body had to cope with a system of great complexity. At the beginning of the twentieth century, there were 188 different railway companies in Britain, and that does not include subdivisions of larger companies such as the Tanat Valley Light Railway, which had already been absorbed into the larger Cambrian Railway.[3] That was not the end of the complication. Apart from the rolling stock run by the companies themselves, many concerns had their own private wagons and sidings. To take just one example from a typical industrial town in northern England, Bolton in Lancashire: it was served by two railway companies, the London & North Western and the Lancashire & Yorkshire, each of which had its own station. There were also forty-one different sidings spread around the town, ranging from the Corporation Gas Works to the Bolton Iron & Steel Co. Deliveries could be made and wagons picked up from any or all of these concerns, either in privately owned or railway company wagons, which meant trains had to be made up with care to make sure that everything arrived and left in the right order. It was a logistic puzzle that had to be solved many times per day on railways all over Britain. Passenger travel might have seemed less complex, but journeys could involve passing over the tracks of many different companies. An individual might buy a ticket from one place to another and have no interest whatsoever in who owned each length of track that the train was crossing over, but it mattered to the companies. Each of them had to have their due share of the ticket price. The job of allocating the appropriate funds from freight and passenger services fell to the Railway Clearing House, established in 1851. It was a cumbersome system in many ways, but it worked. One reason that it worked was that the railways employed a vast workforce, with even modest stations having a large staff. Whatever its shortcomings it represented the most important system that the country had for moving goods and people, and it was at the forefront of technological advance.

When the first railways were built, scientific 'experts' prophesied all kinds of horrors. The magnificently named Dr Dionysius Lardner had declared that because the lines in Box tunnel on the Great Western were on a gradient, trains travelling down the slope would emerge at a speed of 120mph, at which velocity no human being would be able to breathe. The fact that the good doctor had neglected to include either friction or air resistance in his calculation, as the company's engineer I.K. Brunel pointed out, didn't of course alter his prognosis of what would happen should such a speed ever be reached. No one had quite got round to testing that in 1914, but ten years previously the locomotive *City of Truro* had achieved a speed of 102mph and no respiratory problems had been reported.

The new governing body had taken over a railway in which locomotive design had produced a range of engines capable of handling all kinds of traffic, from the fast passenger express to little tank engines that spent their working lives shunting wagons around marshalling yards. Rolling stock had also been improved, including goods wagons. For example, in 1900 the North Eastern Railway had only two wagons capable of holding over 12 tons, but by the start of the war had 18,000 of them. The raw material was there and the technology was well developed: the big question was how to make the best use of them. Not only was the rolling stock spread out between the different companies, but almost half of the country's 1.5 million wagons were privately owned. It was a daunting task to bring everything together to serve the needs of war.

Making efficient use of goods trains was an urgent priority. There were a number of established practices that did nothing at all to increase efficiency. Because of the multiplicity of companies it was quite common for freight that had to cross company borders to be transferred from its original set of wagons to ones belonging to the owner of the new territory. This was easily dealt with by new regulations. A far less tractable problem was caused by the existence of the vast fleet of privately owned wagons. For years they had been regarded as a nuisance by the big companies, partly because they had no control over the quality and design of wagons, but more seriously because of the huge inefficiencies involved. The Railway Executive was well aware of the problem and quoted a typical example of wasteful, uneconomic practice:

> In one instance, at least, a colliery company sending coal in their own wagons to a certain port refused permission to the railway company to make use of those wagons for the conveyance to them of hay for the ponies in their own collieries, the railway company being compelled to return the coal wagons empty and provide another set of wagons for the hay going to the same destination.[4]

This was clearly not acceptable when the whole railway system was being put under immense strain. It was not just the sudden increase in traffic that caused the problem. The companies had been ordered to supply 20,000 wagons for use in France. Somehow the stock had to be replaced, and the most obvious solution was to commandeer private wagons. An act was passed in December 1916 enabling the Railway Board to 'take possession of any private owner's wagons and to use them as they think best in the interests of the country as a whole'. It sounded a good idea in theory, but did not work out in practice. The private owners' wagons were a hotchpotch of different styles, many of them colliery wagons, specifically designed for the loading and discharge of coal, but not much use for general purposes. The best that could be done was to control the use of wagons in a specific area to make the system as efficient as possible. This worked very well in the major coalfields, such as Durham and South Wales. This was particularly important for Wales whose collieries were famous for providing what was known as 'steam coal', coal of a very high calorific value, particularly valuable for use in ships. At the height of the war, 100 trains per week were running to the Grangemouth Docks on the Firth of Forth for the use of the fleet, carrying some 400,000 tons of coal.

Coal was such an important commodity, being essential for the running of industry and the heating of millions of homes, that regulations were brought in to ensure that it was moved around the country as efficiently as possible. In 1917 the most severe restrictions were imposed using Defence of the Realm Regulations. The aim was to keep to a minimum the distance that the coal had to be moved. To achieve this, the country was divided up into twenty districts and no one was allowed to move coal from one district into another without the permission of the Controller of Mines.

Sorting out the problems of goods traffic did not just involve freight trains and marshalling yards; a lot of traffic went through local stations. Even a modest local station would have its own goods shed and sidings. Customers expected wagons to be available to move material brought to the station or they would send their own wagons to be added to a train. Everything had to be sorted out, which was a complex business, to ensure that all the wagons were attached to the correct train and in the right order. At the medium-sized stations horses could be used to move the trucks around the sidings, while at bigger concerns small shunting engines were kept busy puffing to and fro.

Not everything was sent by goods trains. A lot of small items went in the guard vans of passenger trains. The railway porter of those days had quite a wide range of jobs to fulfil. Passengers expected someone to be available to carry their luggage to and from the train: the tip was an important supplement to wages. Wily porters knew that the first-class generally had the heaviest luggage but paid the lightest tips. As an old porter told the author many years ago: 'Folk like them didn't get rich by giving it to folk like us.' But that was only a part of the duties. As each train arrived there would be barrows and trollies full of items, all labelled with their destinations, to load on board and others to be taken off. Mailbags and newspapers were among the items sent every single day of the year, but the rest was a miscellany of objects from modest parcels to bulky items. In the war years, staff shortages became ever more acute. Drivers and firemen were too valuable to be called up for military service – though some were sent to France to drive the military trains. The biggest staff shortages, however, were among the ordinary station workers. As early as June 1915 it was clear that there was a limit to what could be handled, so a rule was brought in that no item weighing more than 3cwt (hundredweight) could be sent by passenger train.

Staff shortages were felt everywhere. The huge increase of traffic meant that locomotives had to be worked harder and harder and that, in turn, meant that less and less time was available for essential maintenance work. As a result, drivers and firemen had a difficult job coaxing good performances out of locomotives that no longer responded to the controls with the smooth efficiency of earlier days. That was only a part of the problem. In pre-war years there were strict regulations covering the maximum loading for each particular class of locomotive. The Midland Railway, for example, had a good all-purpose workhorse in its Class 2 locomotives that were officially never supposed to haul loads in excess of 180 tons, yet on one occasion at least one of these little engines was recorded as pulling a goods train of 400 tons. This was not just a strain on the locomotive, but a challenge to the crew. In those days there was no through braking on goods trains, with the majority of trains being made up of wagons loosely coupled together. When the train slowed, accelerated or stopped, only the engine and the brake van could control the movement. Each truck moved under its own momentum. Sudden movement when accelerating might cause a coupling to snap under the strain; in stopping there was the danger of one truck moving too violently into the one in front. It took a great deal of skill to control a long goods train, but the job was done.

Passenger traffic also showed an increase during the war years: by the middle of 1917 it was up by roughly 60 per cent over what it had been in 1914. A large proportion of this was due to movement of members of the armed services, both being sent to the battle zones and coming home, some on leave and a depressingly large number with injuries. Special ambulance carriages were developed. The military gave their own designs to the companies, with slightly different versions being asked for by the army and the navy. The first ambulance train for the navy was ordered shortly after the start of the war and was built at the London & North Western railway works at Wolverton. Adapted from existing passenger coaches, it was delivered to Chatham within thirty hours, to the delight of the Surgeon General, Sir James Porter: 'Royal Naval Corridor Ambulance Train from Wolverton has arrived to-day, and has gladdened me very much. It is so satisfactory that I am asking the Admiralty for a second of similar construction. I consider great praise is due for the manner the department under your care has carried out this work.'

The existing facilities at stations were often hopelessly inadequate for dealing with this huge movement of people. This was recognised and public-spirited individuals and organisations decided to do something about it, starting in the Scottish Highlands. Perth was a station serving three lines, the Caledonian, the North British and the Highland and soon became a collecting point for soldiers. Within days of the start of the war, local women started arriving with baskets of fruit for the troops and then began to serve cups of tea. They decided it would be much more efficient if they had some sort of trolley so that they could serve refreshments on a regular basis. What started as the Perthshire Women's Patriotic Committee quickly became the Barrow Executive Committee. Soon there were enough volunteers to run a twenty-four-hour service, and the station master made a special rest room available between 8 p.m. and 1 a.m., which proved a real boon for the men who had previously nowhere to go while they waited for a connection late at night. It was a vast improvement over hanging around on a cold, draughty platform in Perthshire in winter.

Other schemes spread through the country. In Exeter women set up the mayoress's depot that provided each soldier with a bag containing a sandwich, a piece of cake, fruit and a packet of cigarettes, each bag costing sixpence. The North Eastern Railway made a former saloon available, but the first proper, specialist buffet for troops was set up in February 1915. The inspiration for it was a letter to *The Times* dated 6.45 a.m., 4 February, and headed 'On leave and very cold':

> Would it not be possible to have at Victoria, and possibly other stations, a heated room for the troops? It is rather unpleasant to arrive here, returning on leave from France, to find all doors closed. At Boulogne the Red Cross Association has a room at the station always open and with a huge supply of tea and coffee for troops passing through. Surely London can do something of the same sort.

Ten days later such a buffet opened, not at Victoria but Euston and, shortly after opening, the queen arrived to give a royal seal of approval to the enterprise. It was a great success, serving 3,000–4,000 men every twenty-four hours. The volunteers who staffed this and similar schemes throughout the country did a great deal to relieve the miseries of soldiers travelling to and from France.

It was inevitable that some railway companies would have a greater share than others of the increased load created by troop movements. The London & South Western and the South East & Chatham had to cope with heavy traffic from military bases such as Aldershot and Salisbury, linking them to Southampton. They were already important companies, running over decent tracks with modern locomotives and rolling stocks. Other lines also found themselves with more traffic than they would have expected in peacetime. The Caledonian Railway linked with the London & North Western at Carlisle to carry traffic on to Glasgow, Edinburgh and Dundee. Because of the dangers to coastal shipping created by the threat from German warships and Zeppelins, more and more goods were sent by train, and even greater traffic was created with the establishment of the huge munitions factories at Gretna and Georgetown (*see* chapter 5). Like many other railways the line was soon carrying military equipment and personnel. Trains were made up of a bewildering variety of rolling stock: carriages for men, superior carriages for officers, trucks for equipment and cattle trucks for horses. Sorting them all out must have been a logistic nightmare, yet in August 1914 the Caledonian managed to dispatch fifty-five trains in just one weekend, over and above running their normal timetable. It was an heroic achievement. But their problems were nothing compared to those suddenly thrust onto the modest Highland Railway.

When it opened for business in 1863 the Highland served the north of Scotland above Perth with lines stretching all the way to Thurso in the north-east, with another branch heading west to Kyle of Lochalsh. Its main income was expected to come from moving livestock: drovers from the furthest north of the region that the railway served were previously taking up to six weeks to move their cattle south to market – the railway could do it in one day. Just four years after opening, on one notable weekend they transported 20,000 sheep. Human passengers were not available in comparable numbers, although there was a steady stream of sporting gentlemen heading for the grouse moors and the Cairngorm Mountains. The line was difficult to build, rising to a summit at over 1,000ft, so a good deal of the line was single track – 230 miles of the 272 miles between Perth and Thurso. Inevitably it was where construction proved most difficult that the single-track sections were to be found, and this included deep, narrow cuttings. The result was that when the inevitable winter snows hit the region these became blocked. The remedy was to link together three locomotives, with a crude snowplough attached to the lead engine. They formed up a mile away from the blockage and at a given signal, each of the drivers would open the regulator and together at full steam they would hurtle into the blockage. It didn't always work and the line could be closed for weeks at a time. The worst ever storm hit the line in the winter of 1880–81. A train got stuck in a blizzard south of Dava station, about midway between Grantown-on-Spey and Inverness. The passengers had to abandon the train and struggle through the snow to the station. When the blizzard eventually died down a work party was sent to try and release the train. The problem was not so much releasing it as finding it: the snow was eventually measured as reaching 60ft above the carriage roofs. A mixed train also got stuck at the other side of Dava station. Again the passengers made it to safety, but the cattle could not be persuaded to leave the comfort of their wagons for the storm outside. They had to be left and inevitably they all died from suffocation beneath the snow. This was the line that in 1914 was expected to provide the main supply route for the fleet at Scapa Flow.

When one thinks of goods being moved around the country in wartime it is easy to think just in terms of personnel, munitions and armaments but there was also an extra strain on the services that people had been inclined to take for granted. One of these was the Royal Mail. For the vast numbers spending their time at Scapa Flow, letters to and from home were a vital link to some sort of normality. An old cruiser, *Impérieuse*, became the floating post office for the fleet and a regular mail service was established through the Euston–Thurso naval special. It left Euston at 6 p.m. and arrived at Thurso at 3.30 a.m. the next morning in time for the boat to Orkney.

The other important base served by the Highland railway was the vital refuelling and naval repair base at Invergordon, north of Inverness. The station at Invergordon was quite modest but suddenly there was a great influx of workers – 6,000 of them. The station staff had to put in immensely long hours, working through from 6 a.m. to 1 a.m. the next day. It was supposed, at least, to be a safe anchorage, but in December 1915 the cruiser *Natal* exploded with the loss of

400 lives. No one ever discovered the cause of the catastrophe. The station continued to be worked as usual.

More and more demands were made on the line. The collieries of Britain had largely relied on imported timber for pit props, but now they had to obtain them from the forests of Scotland, which meant yet more work for the beleaguered Highland line. One of their more unusual jobs came with the arrival of three Russian ships in Scotland, and the railway had the job of transporting some 300 refugees and 3,000 mainly Russian soldiers. In folklore, the Russians were easily recognised by the snow on their boots.

The extra work took a heavy toll on the railway and, with engines regularly overworked and with no time available for regular maintenance, the situation soon became desperate. By the end of August 1915 the company that had started with 152 engines had been forced to scrap fifty that were totally wrecked and had another fifty waiting for urgent repairs. The executive had to call in twenty engines from other lines and arrange for some of the crippled Highland stock to be sent away for repairs. It is a miracle that the line was able to cope at all. At the end of the war, Sir Herbert A. Walker, acting chairman of the Railway Executive wrote, 'I think the Highland has been hit more than any other company.' No one could disagree. Its operation was only made possible because of the wholehearted support of every single person who worked on the line.

Under the early agreement with the unions, pay was to be settled by arbitration with the government. In 1915 they agreed a war bonus scheme, which gave workers an extra two to three shillings per week if they were over 18. Later it was extended to the younger age group as well, who got 1s 6d per week. The top bonus would be the equivalent of roughly £7 per week at today's prices. The rates went up later in the year, at which point the unions agreed not to ask for any further increases and 'they will not give countenance or support either to a demand on the part of any of their members to re-open the negotiations now made or to any strike that might be entered into in furtherance of their demand'.[5] Half of that bargain was kept in that there were no strikes or threats of strikes, but as the war dragged on prices rose relentlessly and the staff were asked to work ever longer hours. It was inevitable that new demands would be made. By 1917 the war bonus had increased to 15s per week for men and 7s 6d per week for boys. The unions kept the no strike bargain, but there was a short-lived unofficial strike in 1918, mostly affecting the Great Western – the staff went back to work without achieving any sort of increase. On the whole, the system seems to have worked well in the rail industry with little acrimony. As will be clear later, the same could not be said of every industry during the war years.

The big railway companies were not simply concerned with running a transport system; they were also major manufacturers. They had immense workshops, where locomotives and rolling stock could be built and repaired. The Great Western Railway, for example, had built its works on what was then a green field site at Swindon and had to build a whole new town to house the growing workforce. The works became famous for the quality of their workmanship: a mechanic trained at Swindon could claim to be as good as any other craftsman and a great deal better than most. It was a huge concern, and one former worker painted a vivid picture of life in the town at the beginning of the war:

> As soon as the ten minutes hooter sounds the men come teeming out of the various parts of the town in great numbers, and by five minutes to six the streets leading to the entrances are packed with a dense crowd of men and boys … It is a mystery where they all come from. Ten thousand workmen! They are like an army pressing forward to battle Tramp! Tramp! Tramp! Still they pour down the street with the regularity of trained soldiers.[6]

Now the great railway works could no longer be left just to carry on the work for which they were designed. They had to use their facilities for all kinds of essential jobs that were totally unconnected with the running of a railway. One of the first demands was for railway workshops to turn out 12,000 stretchers. The companies made it clear from the start that they would do this type of work at cost, with no extra profit for themselves. But as the war progressed the railway workshops were increasingly involved in many other forms of manufacture that had nothing to do with the railways, helping to fulfil the increasing demand for munitions and ordnance. They were invaluable simply because they already possessed some of the country's most modern machine tools and a workforce highly skilled in their use. Time and effort spent on fulfilling those orders was time that was not available for the regular work of keeping the railways running. By the time peace was declared, the railways were limping along with increasingly battered and worn stock and increasingly exhausted staff. But they kept going and the government showed its appreciation in an official report:

> The success that has attended the operation of the railways throughout the war, which has been superior to that witnessed in any other of the belligerent countries, affords conclusive proof of the adequacy of the arrangements that had been made in advance and of the capacity of those who have been concerned with their execution.
>
> There has been little dislocation, notwithstanding that, in addition to a very large Government traffic, the volume of civilian traffic both of passengers and goods, has been heavier than in pre-war days, that large numbers of the staff have been inexperienced and that considerable demands have been made upon the railways for rolling stock and materials for use with the armies abroad.[7]

The praise was well earned, but the official report suggests a smoothness of operation that it was not always possible to maintain. The report referred to both 'increased traffic' and 'inexperienced staff'. It was perhaps inevitable that given such a combination, accidents would happen. On 22 May 1915 there was a catastrophic collision, in what was to be the worst disaster ever to happen on the British rail system throughout its entire history.[8] The events themselves are complicated, but the problems started when two express trains that had left Euston at 11.45 p.m. and midnight were reported as being late. The signalman at Quintinshill, near Gretna Junction on the

Caledonian Railway, received the information and was told that because of the delay, a local, slow train that would normally have followed the express trains would be sent on ahead. When it reached Quintinshill it was to be shunted into a loop off the main line to allow the express trains through. There were loops on both the down and up lines and one of these was already occupied by a goods train, so the local was switched to the up main line, out of the path of the express trains. Then another train arrived on the up line, an empty coal train that was placed in the other loop. The signalman now also accepted a troop train on the up line. There were now three trains at Quintinshill, one in each of the loops and the third on the up main line. There were also two express trains approaching from the south and a troop train coming from the north. The situation was confused, and confusion was compounded by the fact that all this was taking place just as one signalman was ending his shift and handing over to his replacement. Even so, if the correct signal procedures had been followed, catastrophe would have been averted. They were not.

At 6.42 a.m. the signalman accepted the troop train into his section. Six minutes later, the troop train hauled at speed by an express locomotive appeared and hit the stationary local train head on. The heavy local engine was driven back 40 yards, the tender fell onto the next track, the coupling broke and the carriages rolled back another 100 yards. The engine of the troop train fell across the track. Because rolling stock was so scarce, the troop train had been made up of old wooden-framed coaches. The impact was so great that the first coach was hurled into the air and ended up in front of the locomotive, while the rest were reduced to matchwood. Many on board the local train had survived the initial crash, simply because the broken coupling had sent their coaches shooting backwards. The driver and fireman of the stationary local had seen the express coming and had been able to leap to safety. Worse, however, was to follow.

Guard Graham, who had been at the back of the local train, rushed out with his flag to warn the approaching express due to arrive from the south that what had been a clear line minutes before was now blocked by wreckage. But there was not enough time: the train hauled by two express locomotives was travelling at full speed. The driver did his best to brake, but the momentum was too great. He ploughed into the wreckage of the first crash. The mayhem was terrible but it was made even worse by what followed. The old coaches of the troop train had been lit by gas. The cylinders were smashed in the debris and the high-pressure gas rushed out and was at once ignited by the red-hot coals from the overturned tender. Flames shot through the flimsy carriages, which were soon ablaze from end to end. Eight lives were lost on board the express and fifty-four were injured; two were killed on board the local train. The greatest death toll was in the troop train, though the exact numbers have never been known, mainly because it was impossible to count the charred bodies of those who died in the inferno. By the best estimates, based on those who were officially known to have boarded the train, it appears that 215 officers and men from the 7th Royal Scots regiment were killed and 191 seriously injured, as well as the driver and fireman. The blame was placed squarely on the two men who were in the Quintinshill box that day, and there is no doubt that they made mistakes. But there were other factors peculiar to wartime that made a terrible situation worse. There was far more traffic on the line than would have been experienced in peacetime. The signalling equipment was not up to the best standards of the day and there was neither time nor money to update it, given the other problems facing the railways as a whole. In normal circumstances the coaches that made up the troop train would have long since been pensioned off and turned into scrap. The war had a deadly role to play even on Britain's railways.

3

WATER TRANSPORT

In the previous chapter we looked at some of the ways in which railway companies were immediately affected by the outbreak of war. But these companies were not limited to running trains up and down railed tracks. Some of them had extensive fleets of passenger ferries, linking British ports to the Continent. One of these companies was the Great Eastern, which had direct links through Harwich to Belgium and the Netherlands. Their ships, like those of other railway companies, were immediately requisitioned by the Admiralty. One of these was the steamer *Dresden*, which already had a place in history, though one still wrapped in mystery. On 29 September 1913 the inventor of the engine that stills bears his name, Rudolf Diesel, boarded the vessel in Antwerp, heading for a meeting in London. He went to his cabin at 10 p.m., requesting a call at 6.15 the next morning. The steward found only an empty cabin: his body was later recovered. No one knows exactly what happened. At the start of the war the vessel was converted into an armed boarding steamer. It is ironical that the ship that saw the end of one of the most illustrious of Germany's inventors, should reach its own end in 1918, victim of a torpedo fired from a U-boat fitted with a diesel engine. It sank with the loss of 224 lives.

The *Dresden* had been converted into a naval vessel, but other steamers were used to carry cargo or passengers, not all of whom were military. They were just as vulnerable to attack, and of the eleven Great Eastern vessels taken over at the start of the war only four survived. Under the German edict of February 1915, the unarmed merchantmen were declared to be legitimate targets anywhere in the waters around Britain. They would have been considered easy prey by U-boat commanders, but some of the intended victims had other ideas. Charles Fryatt had made his way through the ranks from seaman to master with the Great Eastern. His life in the early war years was typical of that of many others who simply carried on with their work:

> Since the beginning of the war he had made 143 passages between Harwich or Tilbury and Rotterdam, maintaining, with his colleagues, the route of the G. E. R. Continental service in spite of unlighted coasts, mines, enemy submarines, aircraft and warships. These men depended on their own strong nerves, their skill, the faithfulness of the good crews under their command, and a hope of the observance of sea-law – a hope that was considerably diminished by the attacks on merchant shipping without warning and without care of life.[1]

On 2 March 1915 Captain Fryatt was in command of a former Great Central Railway steamer, the 1,400-ton *Wrexham* built in 1902, when he was spotted by a U-boat and ordered to stop. Instead he ordered all available hands to the engine room to stoke the boilers and get every ounce of steam they could. The theoretical maximum speed of the *Wrexham* was 13 knots but somehow they managed to get that up to 16 knots. They were chased for 40 miles before making it safely into the harbour at Rotterdam. The evidence of the hard work that the crew had put in to maintain this speed could be seen in their soot-blackened faces, and in the blistered paintwork of the funnel, where the flames from the boiler had shot up it.

On 28 March Fryatt was in command of the Great Eastern vessel *Brussels*, of similar size and age to the *Wrexham*, when he was again spotted by a U-boat. This time he decided to go on the offensive and ordered rockets to be fired from the deck to try to convince the Germans that he was heavily armed. The ruse worked and the U-boat promptly submerged. Rather than running away, the captain ordered his ship to steam straight at the periscope that could be seen above the waves. The victim had become the attacker. The *Brussels* hit the U-boat, which was damaged and, listing badly, was forced to retire. It was just as well that Fryatt took an aggressive attitude instead of obeying the U-boat command. That same day an Elder Line ship was also ordered to stop, did so and was blown up before anyone had a chance to escape.

Captain Fryatt's luck ran out in June 1916. This time he was confronted by German destroyers, which he could neither outrun nor attack. The passengers were allowed to leave, but the ship and its captain were taken. Instead of being treated as a prisoner of war he was put on trial as a civilian who had deliberately attempted to ram a German submarine. The trial lasted no more than a few hours. He was found guilty and executed by firing squad the same day. The German Commandant Von Schröder who signed the order wrote: 'A perverse action has thus received its punishment, tardy, but just.' Britain was outraged that a captain could be executed for attempting to defend his ship from enemy attack, and a bronze plaque was placed in Fryatt's memory at Liverpool Street Station, the London terminus of the Great Eastern Railway.

The ferry service offered by the railways was only available for foot passengers, but there was a great demand for vehicles to be sent from England to France. The authorities were anxious to keep at least some of their movements secret. So they opened what became known as Q Port at Richborough near Sandwich, coincidentally very close to the spot where the Saxons had first invaded Britain. It was here that the military adapted old sea-going barges into what were, in effect, the very first roll-on roll-off (ro-ro) ferries for taking vehicles across the Channel. It was a very effective system, but it took a surprisingly long time after the war for this idea to be developed into the familiar ro-ro ferries of today.

Considering the importance of shipping to the national effort, it is surprising that the government made no attempt to direct it until there was a change in leadership, and Lloyd George became prime minister. He set up a Ministry of Shipping and persuaded Sir Joseph Maclay to take charge. Maclay was not a politician but a Glasgow shipowner who, as the senior partner of Maclay & McIntyre, ran a fleet of fifty ships from the Clyde. He took over his new role as minister in December 1916. From the first, he had problems with the Admiralty, who still regarded their role as being to fight great battles at sea and were insisting on giving precedence to building warships, rather than merchantmen to replace the vessels being sunk by the Germans. In June 1917 he warned the government that relations between the Admiralty and the merchant service had become so bad that unless there were reforms 'we shall have these men refusing to go to sea'. Lloyd George also noted that Maclay had 'repeatedly pressed that convoys should be given a trial'.[2]

Maclay proved an effective minister. He used his office to ensure that ships were used to their greatest advantage by controlling what they carried, reducing the amount of non-essential imports. He managed to change the policy on shipbuilding, so that it was finally possible to get more merchantmen built. Perhaps his greatest achievement was to finally persuade the Admiralty that the only answer to the submarine threat was to send ships in escorted convoys. By that action alone he saved the lives of thousands of seamen. At the end of the war, Lloyd George described him as 'a truly wonderful man'.

It is remarkable that some sort of regular service between Britain and Continental ports was continued in spite of the all too evident dangers. Essential cargoes still got through but the bulk of cross-Channel journeys were those involving troopships. Southampton was the main embarkation port, with a total of over 8 million men and their equipment leaving for France. There was also the tragically regular traffic in hospital ships from France, bringing back the wounded, mainly to Dover. The ships were protected by the Dover Patrol, part of which consisted of converted trawlers manned by fishermen who sought to keep the Channel free of mines. Some 2,000 of these volunteers died performing this essential but dangerous work. In 1917 the losses to shipping were so great, with as many as 400 vessels being sunk every month, that there was real concern that Britain could be starved into submission. It was only then that Maclay's pleas were finally heeded and a proper convoy system was instituted, which included the use of airships to act as lookouts for U-boats and other enemy craft. The role played by the merchant marine was officially recognised when those who had manned boats going through war zones were given a special medal, the Mercantile Marine War Medal: 133,135 were awarded.

Inland waterways also played their part during the war years. Long before the outbreak of war, many had already been bought up and were being run by railway companies. They represented 1,360 out of 4,670 miles of navigable waterways and included such major routes as the Kennet & Avon and the Shropshire Union. They automatically came under government control at the same time as their parent railway companies, were subject to the same rules and regulations and also benefited from the war bonus schemes and other incentives. Canal workers on railway-owned routes were exempt from call-up into the army.

The independent canals suffered by comparison. Repair yards had to be closed due to lack of workers and boats were laid up. While railway freight charges were kept low by the government, the canal companies had no choice in the face of rising costs but to raise their charges. As a result they became ever less competitive as old customers turned to other means of transport. The Railway Executive was aware of the problem and although they had no jurisdiction over the canals they wrote to the Minister of Munitions in December 1916:

> We think the time has come when the Ministry of Munitions should take in hand the question of the better use of canals throughout the country for the transport of raw materials used in the manufacture of munitions of war. There must be considerable opportunity for relieving the railway companies by this method.[3]

Later that month there was a meeting at which the canal companies explained that they were having difficulty keeping the system going because of manpower shortages. It was not just men who were going off to war; others were leaving for better-paid work in places such as munitions factories. They wanted to be on the same footing as the railway-owned canals, but it took a year before the Canal Control Committee was in place. By then over 1,000 boats were lying idle for want of crew, with cargo-carrying falling by as much as 100,000 tons per month. The government finally took control over most of the rest of the system, including all the more important routes. The task now was to win back the customers that had been lost.

The problem was that the canals had been built in the eighteenth century and many of them still relied on the narrowboats, able to carry no more than 30 tons each, and the vast majority were still pulled along by horses. There had been a small amount of mechanisation in the nineteenth century when steam narrowboats were introduced, but they never became popular. One problem was that they needed to have space provided for the engine and its supply of coal, and because the boats could not be enlarged – they were designed to fit snugly into the existing locks – valuable cargo space had to be sacrificed. A far more useful development came with the arrival of the simple diesel engine, designed by Swedish engineer Erik Bolinder. One of the new engines was fitted to a Thames lighter in 1910 and proved successful, but at the start of the war only a few boats were equipped with Bolinders. It is perhaps not too surprising that many customers who had started using the railways – that could deliver bigger loads far more quickly and, thanks to government subsidies at lower rates – were reluctant to turn back to the canals.

Some canals did benefit. The Basingstoke had been in a fairly wretched condition at the start of the war, but it ran conveniently close to the big army camp at Aldershot. The Royal Engineers took charge of it and used it to bring in supplies that had been sent down the Thames by barge from the arsenal at Woolwich. The authorities may not have shown any real enthusiasm for using the canals, but they did recognise that in Europe there was a very modern, efficient waterways system that could take a vast amount of cargo for the military, provided the military were able to use it. So soldiers were sent to the British canals to take courses in boat handling. It might have been more efficient to have used all the men who had left the canals to join the army and who required no further training, but that was not the military method of doing things. What eventually emerged was the Inland Waterways Battalion that saw service in France and Belgium, largely working with boats sent over from England.

Other crews worked on the English system itself. On 19 November 1917 a steamer with six boats passed through the locks at Bank Newton on the Leeds & Liverpool Canal.[4] The flotilla was being manned by twenty soldiers under the command of a sergeant. They did not endear themselves to the regular boatmen, mostly because the sergeant insisted that he had priority at all locks. The ordinary boatmen were paid by results: the faster they made a journey the sooner they got paid, and the sooner they were available to take another load. In peacetime locks were used on a strictly first come, first served basis which, while it led to the occasional scuffle over who had actually got there first, was a system that worked well. Being forced to wait rankled, but no one was going to argue with twenty soldiers.

The steamer was used as a floating mess and came complete with an army cook, and the army fleet became a regular sight on the canal. In time more crews were added, but even at its peak the army contingent only supplied thirty-seven men out of nearly 500 working the Leeds & Liverpool. By the end of the war it was recognised that this was not the best way to use skilled men, and soldiers were seconded off to work as mates with regular canal boat captains.

Before the war a certain amount of interest had been shown in the idea of using canals for pleasure. It was not exactly a new idea. As early as 1765 the promoters of the Trent & Mersey Canal had issued a pamphlet extolling the commercial benefits that the waterway would bring, and had also added a paragraph at the end on the delights that a canal could provide:

And if we add the amusements of a pleasure-boat that may enable us to change the prospect, imagination can scarcely conceive the charming variety of such a landscape. Verdant lawns, waving fields of grain, pleasant groves, sequestered woods, winding streams, regular canals to different towns, orchards whose trees are bending beneath their fruit, large towns and pleasant villages, will all together present to the eye a grateful intermixture of objects, and feat the fancy with ideas equal to the most romantic illusions.[5]

No one paid much attention to such ideas at the time, though today we accept canal travel as delightful and relaxing. One of the more popular canals with today's holidaymakers is the Kennet & Avon. The authorities had become responsible for this canal from the start of the war, as it had long since been bought up by the Great Western Railway. Theoretically the company was supposed to keep it in good order; in practice they had very little interest in it. For much of its length, canal and railway ran close together, and GWR engine drivers looked down with lordly scorn on the barges and plodding horses. But it was and is a most attractive waterway, running through some beautiful countryside. The military accepted the idea that canal trips might be just the thing to cheer up convalescing soldiers, so they agreed to allow the Red Cross to run a converted canal boat for the injured men.

The canals may have played a comparatively small role in transport compared with the railways, but it was not insignificant. Records were taken for one month, in July 1916, and showed that boats had carried a very respectable 1.7 million tons. Without their work that would have added a big burden to the already overstretched roads and railways.

In all the discussion of transport in this and the previous chapter, nothing has been said about the roads and road traffic. This seems odd today as we live in an age when so much freight is moved by road. But at the outbreak of the First World War, the motor industry was still in its infancy. There were little more than 80,000 goods vehicles in the whole of the country. Speeds were limited to 20mph and few trucks could carry more than 4 tons. For long-distance haulage they could scarcely compete with the canals, let alone the railways. Horse-drawn traffic was still the norm: it was estimated that in London less than 20 per cent of all commercial traffic was carried in motor vehicles, the rest still being moved by horses.

The number of commercial vehicles in civilian use never increased during the war. Altogether there were fewer private vehicles on the road at the end of the war than there had been at the beginning. A typical advert of the period from truck manufacturer Commer offered 4- or 5-ton vehicles, but they were only available to companies involved in war work.[6] There were severe petrol shortages and early in the war the tax on fuel was doubled. Some owners of trucks and vans involved in what was considered unessential work tried to find alternative fuels. One variation was to strap a huge bag filled with town gas to the top of the vehicle and use that as the fuel. Not surprisingly, it was never a popular solution. Many more vehicle owners simply laid up their vehicles for the duration of the war.

None of this meant that manufacturers stopped making vehicles, just that the vast majority of those that were made went to the military. This will be dealt with in more detail later in Chapter 9. One thing that all transport industries within the country had in common was a serious and growing shortage of workers. This turned out to be a problem with an obvious, but revolutionary, solution.

4

WORK FOR WOMEN

As the war progressed, and the first Christmas came and went with no sign of the promised victory, more and more men were recruited into the armed services. The inevitable result was growing manpower shortages in essential industries. However, there was a very large proportion of the population who were available and keen to do their bit and prepared to tackle all kinds of different jobs: women. Traditionally, women had worked in large numbers in the textile industry, but by far the largest numbers were employed as domestic servants. It is difficult for us today to comprehend the sheer numbers of domestic servants at work in Britain when the war started. The 1911 census covering England and Wales revealed that there were 1,302,438 in service, making this by far the largest group of men or women to work in any single industry, including agriculture. Among the female workers, there were the few of comparatively high status – cooks, housekeepers, nannies and governesses – but by far the greatest numbers were the humble maids. Theirs was a life of almost unrelieved drudgery, rising early in the morning to light fires, prepare meals and start the endless round of cleaning, and often having to stay up until the last of the employers had gone to bed, just in case anyone chose to call on them to perform some task or other. Most had no more than half a day off per week and the lowest paid, such as scullery maids, could be earning no more than 5s per week (roughly £12 at today's prices). It is no wonder that many of them would welcome a chance to do anything else that was offered. And they were not the only poorly paid women who welcomed a new opportunity: tens of thousands more were employed in the sweatshops of the rag trade. What was needed was an initiative that would open the doors for these women and allow them into what had been a virtually all-male world.

In the first five months of the war, there was considerable propaganda to suggest that women should enrol for war work, and it was strongly suggested that keeping them on in 'unproductive' jobs such as domestic service and the clothing industry was somehow unpatriotic. As a result, a large number of women were sacked but, unfortunately for them, no one had yet worked out where and how they were to be employed in the industrial world. The one area where there was a notable increase in the use of women was in clerical work. During most of the nineteenth century, male clerks had been employed, writing letters by hand and, in most large concerns, copying them into a letter book. The first typewriter had been introduced early in the century, described by its inventor as being capable of writing 'almost as fast as by hand', but it was not until the end of the century that the modern typewriter appeared, with the familiar 'shift' key that enabled the same keyboard to be used for both upper-case and lower-case letters. The male clerk was beginning to give way to the female typist. The war led to a definite increase in this type of work, but had little impact on the vast majority of potential female workers, many of whom lacked the necessary literacy skills.

The suffragettes were among the earliest campaigners for the greater use of women in war work. As soon as it was announced in August 1914 that all the suffragettes who had been jailed for their protests were to be released, their leader, Emmeline Pankhurst announced that they would stop campaigning for votes. She hoped that women would be able to use their influence to work towards peace, but would support the war effort. Two other suffragettes, Decima Moore and Evelina Haverfield, set up a voluntary body to help the armed forces, the

Women's Emergency Corps. As members were required to pay £2 to join, and provide their own uniforms, it was necessarily a very elitist organisation. It did not even receive the support of all the suffragettes, for there was a strong pacifist element among the leading members of the movement who opposed the war. But the overall tone was of jingoistic patriotism that characterised so much of society in those years. Christabel Pankhurst came back to Britain, after an exile of two and a half years, and issued a rousing proclamation:

> The people of this country must be made to realise that this is a life and death struggle, and that the success of the Germans would be disastrous for the civilisations of the world, let alone for the British Empire.
>
> Everything that we women have been fighting for and treasure would disappear in the event of a German victory. The Germans are playing the part of savages, overwhelming every principle of humanity and morality, and taking us back to the manners and methods of the Dark Ages.[1]

There was no doubt that Christabel Pankhurst's patriotism was heartfelt, but she must also have been very well aware that for years the suffragettes had been reviled as little better than demented revolutionaries. Now she could try a different approach by declaring a unilateral truce in the fight for votes as being in the national interest: in place of the old struggle the movement would have a new battle to get women their share of essential war work. The motives may not have been entirely patriotic. If women could be shown as capable of doing work previously reserved for men, then the case for being given the vote would be all the stronger. Women had found roles as volunteers in organisations such as the Women's Legion set up by the Marchioness of Londonderry in July 1915, and had proved very effective. What had not happened was the opening up of the industrial world to women, not as volunteers taking on traditional feminine roles but as workers capable of being taught crafts and skills. One obstacle appeared to be the opposition of the unions, but that vanished in March 1915 when they volunteered to end restrictions on using women and unskilled labour, accepting what became known as 'dilution'.

A major factor in the change of heart was the fact that the unions trusted Lloyd George, who was seen as a 'man of the people'. Unlike grandees such as Herbert Asquith, the former prime minister, Lloyd George had come through the State education system and had already shown himself to be a radical reformer. Now in charge of munitions, he was eager to get the new system under way, and set up the women's war register. Posters were put up with stirring slogans: 'Do your Bit, Replace a Man for the Front'. Thousands of women responded, eager to take up the challenge. But inevitably the process became somewhat bogged down in committees and meetings, much to the frustration of the women who were ready to help.

On 24 June 1915, Emmeline Pankhurst delivered a rousing speech at London Polytechnic that set out her case in the strongest possible terms and is worth quoting at some length:

Women are eating their hearts out with desire to see their services utilised in this national emergency. It is not a question with us of war bonuses; it is not a question of red tape, which has to be slowly untied. With us it is not a question of these things; but we realise that if this war is to be won, the whole energy of the nation and the whole capacity of the nation will have to be utilised in order to win.

And that is not the opinion of women alone; the Prime Minister said it weeks ago; Mr. Lloyd George has said it. But what is the outcome of all they have said? A week is to be spent and perhaps a minimum of money is to be spent on getting a comparatively small number of men trade unionists into line on this question … How is it that men can be so behind as not to see that the fire of patriotism burns in the hearts of women quite as strongly as it does in the hearts of men.

Imagine what women are thinking, when they find in Germany half a million women today are engaged in making ammunition – while 70,000-odd women who registered themselves at Easter at one single invitation of the Board of Trade are only being utilised to the number of 2,000 for national service …

I expect I'm the biggest rebel in this meeting and I am one of the biggest rebels in the country. I am one of those people who, at the right time and in the proper place, are prepared to fight for certain ideals of freedom and liberty and would be willing to give my life for them; we are prepared to hold great organising meetings all over the country and enlist women for war service if they will only set us free to do it. We here and now this afternoon offer our services to the Government, to recruit and enlist the women of the country for war service, whether that war service is the making of munitions or whether, that war service is the replacing of skilled men who have been called up, so that the business of the country can go on.[2]

There was continued opposition to women moving into the factories and other workplaces, mainly from the skilled men, worried about their own loss of status. The trade unions may have reached agreement, but not all their members were equally enthusiastic. Emmeline Pankhurst continued to press for change. She was still fighting the same fight in October 1915, months after the agreement between Lloyd George and the unions. 'Yes, there is opposition there, opposition and prejudice of a kind almost intolerable in time of peace, but which is something like treachery and traitorism in time of war.' But although advances were being made in a number of different industries, it was on the strict understanding that this was all a temporary arrangement. The agreement between the National Union of Railwaymen, the employers and the government, made in August of that year, was quite specific and typical of many other similar documents:

An assurance was asked for and given that the employment of women in capacities in which they had not formally been employed was an emergency provision arising out of circumstances created by the war, and would not prejudice in any way any undertaking given by the companies to re-employment of men who had joined the Colours on the conclusion of the war.[3]

One of the first railway jobs taken over by women was as ticket collectors, but soon they were doing all the jobs around the station, though some prejudice remained among the public at first. There were complaints that having a woman call out the name of the station was 'unfeminine'; and wearing breeches, even when they were the only practical garments for the work involved, was definitely frowned upon. The women soon proved their worth, moving on to jobs that would previously have been considered totally unsuitable, including plate laying and track maintenance. They also began to move into jobs with considerable responsibility, such as guards on trains. Even so, it is still surprising to find a photograph taken in 1917 at Irlams O'th Heights Station, Manchester, in which two female porters pose alongside a female station master.

Women found work throughout the transport industry. They provided crews for buses and trams – drivers and conductresses; they drove vans of all kinds, including mail vans. This was at a time when the internal combustion engine was comparatively new and technology had not advanced very far. Starting a vehicle was not just a matter of turning a key or pressing a button, it involved taking out the starting handle to get the engine turning over. This was hard work – and not without its dangers. It was very easy for the handle to jerk backwards, which could lead to a sprained or even broken wrist. Film shot during the period showed women in all kinds of operations, from filling wagons at collieries to driving steamrollers. Some even worked as navvies. Throughout industry, they proved that, given the opportunity, they were capable of doing virtually any job that a man could do. Doing equal work, however, did not mean equal pay. Once the employment of women had been accepted as a normal part of wartime life, the suffragettes began a new campaign for equal pay. Their magazine, *The Woman's Dreadnought*, was full of letters complaining about the problem. This is an extract from a letter merely signed 'A Munitions Worker':

The first few women who entered the factory at which I work in Croydon (Government Contractors) received 12*s* 6*d* a week, with the bait held out to them that under the premium bonus system which is in vogue the women would be able to earn £1 a week.

The new hands they are taking on are only to receive 8s. a week, with a promise that when they know their work they will have a raise!!!???

Take off the insurance 3d., and unemployment contributions 5d., and that reduces the women's wages horribly – already the women are coming to me to say they cannot live on them – some have children to keep.[4]

Rallies were held, many supported by trade unionists. One in Trafalgar Square was advertised under the banner headlines 'Down with sweating! If a woman does a man's job she must have a man's pay! Down with high prices and big profits'. It was to be a long struggle that met with only mixed success.

By 1916 the work being done by women was officially recognised. The War Office put out a statement in September of that year noting that employers who had recruited women 'readily admit that the results achieved by the temporary employment of women far exceed their estimates, and even so are capable of much further extension'. It went on to declare that no men who were eligible for military service should be kept in civilian employment if a woman could do the job instead. And it soon became clear they were able to turn their hands to practically any job. An article in *The Engineer* described work done by women in the armaments industry in glowing terms and was quite scathing about the men in engineering who considered that 'women are only capable of doing repetition work on foolproof machines'. It went on to give examples of exactly the sort of highly skilled jobs they had mastered:

Quite a large number of girls were able to set up and grind their own tools, and a small proportion could set up their jobs from drawings. They could mill all the parts of the breech mechanism of howitzers, screwing the internal thread for the breech block, milling the interrupted screw, and screwing the cone that fits into the breech block;

milling fire pins, and all the parts of gun sights; in each case setting up their own work.[5]

In other words, some of these girls and women could understand engineering drawings and work directly from them without further instruction. They were setting up and operating complicated machine tools. They were doing work that would normally have only gone to a man who had served a full apprenticeship. Wartime conditions had not given them that luxury: they had to learn quickly and learn well.

Even as late as 1917, there were companies where men rebelled against the employment of women. A company in Castleton, Lancashire sacked men who refused to show women how to work machinery. The firm announced that it had never accepted trade unions nor given in to any demands of the workers, and had no intention of starting now. It seems, however, that they had been altogether too high-handed. When the sacked men took their case to a tribunal, the judgement was that the company had not explained the position to the men in advance, and judgement went against them and they were fined £35 with 25 guineas costs.

The women were undoubtedly proud of their own efforts and had their own monthly magazine, *The War Worker*, the cover of which showed a munitions worker and a soldier standing side by side, each holding a Union Jack. The world was changing: even some office workers felt that they could serve the nation better by working in a factory than they could by working in a typing pool. A correspondent to *The Times* wrote that in some offices men were actually having to type their own letters or write them by hand as the staff deserted them for work that was more interesting, more worthwhile to the war effort and, not unimportantly, better paid. The Chief Woman Inspector of the Board of Trade Labour Exchange spelt out exactly what was happening:

Women love substitution jobs: there is a patriotic glamour about replacing men which is not to be found in the normal pre-war occupations of women. This enthusiasm has another side, and it is the cause of the distinct unpopularity of obvious female occupations such as dress-making and millinery, and the difficulty which business firms needing such workers find in obtaining them.[6]

There was another aspect that was put forcibly in the letter pages of *The Times*. The women who had rushed to volunteer for war work 'are not going to accept domestic service at any price'.[7] The days when the big houses could confidently expect to hire a large staff on the cheap were coming to an end.

The militant suffragettes had suffered greatly in their fight to get the vote but with very little success. But when the issue was again raised in Parliament, the decisive factor was that women had proved themselves in war work and to deny them the vote no longer made any sense, if it ever had done. There was still opposition, but even Asquith, who had been an opponent for the movement, had a change of heart: 'Some years ago I ventured to use the expression. "Let the women work out their own salvation." Well, Sir, they have worked it out during this war.'[8] The move to give women the vote was approved by the Commons and then by the Lords in January 1918.

It was not just a fact that women helped in the war effort; it would be more accurate to say that Britain could never have won without them. During the first year of the war, 382,000 women entered the workforce, and the following year there was a further 563,000, after which, inevitably, the numbers slightly fell away. Nevertheless, by 1918 women made up almost half the total workforce.[9] They changed the whole industrial landscape, and nowhere was this truer than in the munitions industry.

5

STIRRING THE DEVIL'S PORRIDGE

British industry should have been able to meet the demands of the military, but in order for that to happen, the military had to have a realistic idea of what would be needed. Unfortunately, that was not the case at the beginning of the war, when the generals were still hoping to fight the battles of the past, with the techniques and technology of the nineteenth century. The attitudes were typified by the views of two of the leading figures, Douglas Haig, who from 1915 was commander-in-chief in France, and Lord Kitchener, who had been made Secretary of War in 1914. At the start of the war, Haig had announced that he thought two machine guns per battalion would be 'more than sufficient'. Kitchener was slightly more ambitious, recommending four, but could not imagine there would ever be any need for more than that. As a result, at the start of the war, the army had a grand total of 1,530 machine guns, but by the end of the war nearly 250,000 had been manufactured. Lloyd George was scathing about the views of the old brigade: 'Take Kitchener's figure. Square it. Multiply by two. Then double again for good luck.'[1]

The importance of machine guns, and their deadly effectiveness, was to become all too apparent during the long years of trench warfare on the Western Front. The other aspect of the generals' strategy was a firm belief that, once the lines of trenches had been established, the enemy positions could be softened up by heavy artillery bombardments to such an extent that it would be possible for foot soldiers to advance across no-man's-land for a successful attack. Repeated failures of this strategy and the huge loss of life that resulted did little to change their minds. Once again, however, the military in the early stages of the war had made no plans for this sort of action, and the result was seen in what became known as the 'Shell Scandal' of 1915. Whether there was a genuine shell problem or not is open to doubt. Sir John French ordered an attack in March of that year at Neuve Chapelle. It pierced the German lines, but the breach was closed before reinforcements arrived. The French blamed the failure on a lack of shells, even though in the initial bombardment the artillery had fired more rounds than they had during the whole of the Boer War. Most military historians blame the failure on a strategy that had no hope of success, throwing troops at a short section of the German lines. However, the issue was seized on by political opponents of the government as all that was needed to launch a campaign against the way in which the war was being managed at home. Kitchener himself admitted: 'I can only say that the supply of war materials at the present moment and for the next two or three months is causing me very serious concern.'[2]

The public was first made aware of the problem by the war correspondent for *The Times*, Lt Col Charles à Court Repington, who had served with the Rifle Brigade in the Boer War. He was horrified by the casualties inflicted on his old regiment during the failed attack on Aubers Ridge and once again blamed the failure on a shell shortage. His report appeared in the newspaper on 14 May under the headline 'Need for Shells: British attack checked. Limited supply the cause'. In the text, Repington specifically stated, 'we had not sufficient high explosives to level the enemy's ramparts to the ground'. The lack of essential artillery support then led to the whole assault being abandoned. But the real campaign for change was led by Lord Northcliffe, through his newspaper the *Daily Mail*. On 21 May it ran a scathing denouncement under the much more dramatic headline

'The Tragedy of the Shells; Lord Kitchener's Grave Error'. But Kitchener was still a hero in the country: the *Mail* readership was not impressed and the newspaper's circulation actually fell. It was quite clear that Kitchener was far too popular to be displaced as Minister of War.

There was, however, a dramatic end to the campaign. A coalition government was formed and Lloyd George was put in charge of a new Ministry of Munitions. The new ministry, in Lloyd George's own words, was 'from first to last a business man organisation'. It set about devising a simple method of costing war work, based on the actual costs plus 'a reasonable profit' and new businesses were promptly established. The effect on the whole munitions industry was dramatic. Thousands of new factories, large and small, were set up, while other existing businesses were converted to supply arms and munitions, including such unlikely candidates as the new HMV gramophone factory. The government paid out £2,000 million to ensure that the guns could keep firing, and by the end of the war controlled a work-force of over 3 million.

The earliest form of shell used in the war was the shrapnel shell, filled with lead balls, a device that took its name from Lt Henry Shrapnel of the Royal Artillery, who developed the first version, based on a hollow cannonball, right back in 1784. The lead balls were manufactured in a shot tower, and were basically similar to, but larger than, the lead shot used in shotgun cartridges, generally about 0.5in in diameter. Molten lead was poured through a steel screen at the top of the tower. As the droplets fell, they met an updraft of air that solidified them, and at the bottom of the tower they dropped into water, completing the hardening process. Lead, being comparatively soft, causes more damage to flesh than a hardened bullet that could pass straight through a part of the body. The idea of the shell was that when it landed an explosive charge sent the lead balls out in all direc-tions at high speed, with the idea of hitting as many of the enemy as possible with just one round. Although it had been used successfully by the British Army for about a century, it proved largely ineffective once the opposing forces had settled down in their trenches: the shell exploded, and the shrapnel simply whistled harmlessly overhead. It was rapidly replaced by the high explosive shell, which, as its name suggests, was filled with explosives that fragmented the whole shell on detonation, with great destructive power.[3]

Both types of shell required similar forms of operation to produce the outer casing, manufactured out of steel. The most common method involved starting with a billet of steel, up to 16ft long, which could be turned on a lathe. It would then be cut into shell lengths, and each shell would then be drilled. The rough casing could then be machined to ensure that it was a perfect fit in the gun barrel, and shaped from the flange at the bottom that would fit into the grooves of the rifled gun barrel to the pointed nose. The shell needed a fuse to detonate it, which would contain a substance such as mercury fulminate that can be detonated by percussion. The typical British 18-pounder was more complex. It also contained a 'gaine', a tube that penetrated deep into the shell, and was filled with three different explosives, each more powerful than the last. The result was that the shell could penetrate deep into the target before the chain reaction in the fuse set off the main explosive charge.

The manufacture of shell casings and fuse parts were all activities that could be undertaken by any precision engineering firm, and companies could readily be turned to the task. In most cases, existing machine tools could be used or adapted, and for a skilled worker it made little difference whether they were turning a shell casing or a crankshaft for an engine. The main area where new works were required was in preparing the explosives and filling and assembling the shells.

One of the main explosives used in Britain was cordite, a mixture of guncotton, nitroglycerine and acetone. Nitroglycerine was developed by Alfred Nobel and is made by a chemical reaction between nitric and sulphuric acids and glycerol. The process needs to be carried out with considerable care, as the product is highly unstable. Guncotton manufacture is a more complex process. It begins with thoroughly cleaning the cotton, bleaching it and untangling the fibres. Nitration takes place when the cotton is added to a vat filled with a mixture of nitric and sulphuric acids. This happens quite quickly, and then the pot is spun to remove most of the acid. The guncotton then has to be boiled up to five times in water to get rid of the last of the acid mixture. It is then removed, cut up into small pieces, and boiled yet again, before finally being dried.

When the ingredients are mixed together, they form a lumpy mass, which has to be vigorously stirred to make a consistent mixture. It was Arthur Conan Doyle who, when watching the making of this deadly substance, coined the phrase – 'stirring the devil's porridge'.

Picric acid was also widely used as an explosive. It was known as lyddite, simply because it was first produced in Britain at Lydd in Kent. It was also made at the Woolwich Arsenal, where a large part of the workforce during the war years consisted of women and girls. Volunteers of the Voluntary Aid Detachments (VADs) helped out, providing various services. One VAD cook, who like many of the other volunteers was clearly from a very different social class from that of the paid workers, kept a diary of her time at the Arsenal:

> The girls are very rough, regular cockneys but mostly amiable if not rubbed the wrong way. If they are it is Billingsgate gone mad. The only thing then is to give it them hot & they generally shut up after a bit. A good many come from the danger buildings. When they arrive at their work they have to take out all hairpins & must not wear metal buttons or hooks & eyes. They have to take off their own shoes on one side of the shift room, & jump over a barrier onto what is called the clean side in their stockinged feet. There they put on danger shoes which are soft and have no tread.[4]

These girls were working filling cartridges for bombs, and the precautions were clearly essential to avoid any chance of a spark setting off an explosion. The VAD cook went on, in a later entry, to describe the actual work:

> I was shown the Lyddite works. This is a bright canary yellow powder (picric acid) & comes to the factory in wooden tubs. It is then sifted. The house, (windows, doors, floor & walls) is bright yellow, & so are

the faces & hands of all the workers. As soon as you go in the powder in the air makes you sneeze & splutter & gives you a horrid bitter taste at the back of the throat. After sifting the acid is put in cans & stood in tanks where it is boiled until it melts into a clear fluid like vinegar. Then it is poured into the shell case. But a mould is put in before it has time to solidify. This mould when drawn out leaves a space down the middle of the shell. Before it is drawn out beeswax is poured in, & then several cardboard washers put in. Then the mould is replaced by a candle-shaped exploder of TNT or some other very high explosive is put in.

   After this the frieze cap is screwed in, & then two screws have to be put in to hold it firm. The holes for these screws must not be drilled straight into the detonator. If they do the thing explodes.

A Pathé Pictorial film shows similar processes in a different munitions factory, starting with a girl catching the early morning train and, just as the previous diary had described, changing into her work clothes, overalls, with her hair tucked away inside a cap. At the end of the day, the whole process was reversed and the girl had to wash away all the dust and chemicals that she might have picked up during the working day, before changing back into her everyday clothes. They also had to wash before meal breaks. Not all factories, it seems, had these facilities. And although the girl in the film looked bright and cheery, there was a darker side to the life of a munitions worker. The same Pathé film showed the girls receiving regular medical inspections, though it was so perfunctory, lasting no more than a few seconds, that it is doubtful whether it could have had much real value. There were genuine health problems that were never addressed. One worker, Mrs Hall, recalled her working days at the Perivale Royal Filling Station:

We got home and had a lovely good wash and, believe me, the water was blood red and our skin from then on, until a twelve-month after the war, was perfectly yellow. Right down through the body – legs and toes, and toe nails even – perfectly yellow.[5]

This earned the girls who worked with lyddite the nickname 'the canaries'. Working with mercury fulminate could produce far worse results than mere staining of the skin: 'The mercury didn't show, it was more deadly to the flesh I think, but it didn't show so much except that if it got to the eyes it would cause mercurial poisoning, which I had.'

In spite of unpleasant and even deadly side-effects, the girls who did this work seem to have been as cheerful as the Pathé film showed. The Hayes Filling Factory No. 7 employed some 10,000 women and girls and they even had their very own song:

> We are the Hayes Munitions girls
> Working night and day
> Wearing the roses off our cheeks
> For very little pay.
> Some people call us lazy
> But we're next to the boys on the sea.
> If it wasn't for the munitions girls
> Where would the Empire be?

There's a certain perkiness about the verse – these are girls who know their worth, even if they didn't think they necessarily got the cash return they might have expected and certainly deserved. Many of the girls who worked at Hayes joined the National Federation of Women Workers (NFWW) set up by Mary Macarthur. She was born in Glasgow in 1880, but the family moved to Ayr where her father opened a shop and became an enthusiastic supporter of the Conservative Party. She was interested in politics and could have followed in the footsteps of a well-known shopkeeper's daughter from Grantham if her father had not sent her to spy on the local Shop Assistants' Union to see if they were planning to demand better wages and conditions from people like himself. The result was not at all what he expected. As she listened to the passionate speeches about the struggles of many shop assistants to gain a living wage, she became convinced that they were in the right. She became an active trade unionist and soon began to rise through the ranks, lending her support to women who struck out for better conditions in industries as varied as the jute manufacturers of Dundee and the chain makers of the Black Country. She was the first general secretary of the NFWW, an active suffragette and an opponent of the war. In spite of this, she was appointed to the Ministry of Labour's committee on women's employment. She had no problem in being, in a sense, on both sides of possible disputes about women's pay – she remained firmly determined to support the union when it demanded better pay. Because of the provisions of the 1915 Munitions of War Act, workers no longer had the right to go on strike, but the union could argue on their behalf and take their case to arbitration. The women at Hayes were getting 3½d per hour for jobs for which men were being paid 6d. They never managed to achieve parity. The same fight for equal pay was supported by the NFWW in a number of war industries as well as munitions.

Government sources tried to paint a picture of a happy, contented workforce with no thought of anything beyond their patriotic duty. They put up posters and even printed postcards with suitably stirring sentiments:

> There's no uniform so dinky
> As the Girls' 'Munition Blue'
> She's working hard for the coming home,
> Of the Boys at the front so true.

No mention here of poor pay and hardship. No mention either of the fatal illnesses contracted by many who worked in the industry: it was estimated that of those who worked with TNT, some 400 died as a direct result of working with dangerous chemicals. But whatever the pay problems, and whatever the dangers of the work, hundreds of thousands of women rushed to join the new factories, and one of the biggest of them all was set up near Gretna Green in Scotland.

This was one of three munitions factories established in Scotland and was to specialise in the manufacture of cordite. It was an immense site, spreading over 9 square miles, and had two small townships that had been specially built to accommodate the workforce.[6] Over 30,000 workers were employed in construction. They built the workshops and facilities for the workers, all of which were constructed of timber. There was a good reason for this. The risk of explosions on such a site are necessarily high, and if something does go wrong, far less damage will be caused when a building made of wood goes up than if it were built of brick or concrete – and, of course, it would be easier and cheaper to replace. Yet the buildings were only a small part of the job. The site was chosen because it already had good transport connection. It was near to the sea for coastal transport and to the main railway line and road linking the Scottish west coast to England. Equally importantly, it was not too close to large conurbations, which again might suffer from a disastrous explosion. But although these transport links were good, the site still needed to have its own road network and 100 miles of internal rail track. It also had its own power station. The total cost was £9 million, of which £1 million went on the communication system, £1.3 million on housing and £1.3 million on the power house. It was to more than prove its worth. The old munitions works, such as the Royal Gunpowder Factory at Waltham Abbey, had been of immense importance in developing the new materials such as guncotton and cordite, but did not have the capacity to produce immense quantities of material. The works at Waltham Abbey was only able to turn out 70 tons of shells per week: Gretna, once it reached full production, produced 1,000 tons per week.

The men who came to build the site at Gretna were described by a contemporary as 'a very poor lot, ill-fed, out-at-elbows and badly booted'. They were regarded with considerable suspicion by many of the locals and rumours were spread that they were all conscientious objectors, 'cowards' who were too scared to do the manly thing and go and fight at the front. In fact, an estimated 5,000 of the workforce came across from Ireland, following a long tradition of navvies crossing the Irish Sea for work. When demands started to appear that they should be conscripted into the army, the Irish immediately threatened to go home unless they were given exemption. They carried on working, and the whole site was open for business within nine months of work starting. It was never prettified and little was spent on luxuries. When Sir Arthur Conan Doyle visited the site he described it as surrounded by 'primeval ooze lying in stagnant pools'. A rather fuller description was given by Rebecca West who visited the site in the autumn of 1916:

> It consists of a number of huts, some like the government built huts for Irish labourers and some like the open air shelters in a sanatorium and scattered over five hundred acres; they are connected by raised wooden gangways and interspersed with green mounds and rush ponds. It is of such vital importance to the State that it is ringed with barbed-wire entanglements and its products must have sent tens of thousands of our enemies to their death. And it is inhabited chiefly by pretty young girls clad in a Red Riding Hood fancy dress of khaki and scarlet.[7]

The green mounds were not there as ornamental features, but to provide a barrier against blasts from any possible explosion. The 'pretty young girls' were, however, indeed little more than girls: statistics show that 60 per cent of the workforce was under the age of 18. There were far more workers needed at Gretna than could be supplied locally, and public speakers were sent out to appeal for volunteers for war work. They had no problem finding enthusiastic girls, who were recruited from many different parts of Scotland, northern England and Wales. A large number came from the Lancashire mills, where work was scarce and pay poor (*see* chapter 14). Women working on making uniform cloth in the woollen mills received a War Bonus, but this was rarely available for those in the cotton mills. A mill worker might earn 15s per week, but could double that by moving to munitions. There were so many different accents to be heard at Gretna that it was described by one commentator as a 'Tower of Babel'. The various groups did not always get on with each other at first, and tended to stay with others from the same regional background. Some of the Scots showed hostility to the English, and told the Sassenachs to get back home, while the English objected to the Welsh getting together and speaking their own language. In time, as they got used to living and working together, the barriers began to tumble. By 1917 there were 11,576 female workers out of a total workforce of 16,642.

Over one-third of the workers had previously been in domestic service. This is not too surprising, since according to the Board of Trade, in the country as a whole 100,000 women and girls had left domestic work for munitions factories by 1916. The story of Nina Cooper was typical of that of many of those who came to work at Gretna. Previously, she had been a servant working sixty hours per week for just 6s. She was now able to earn 22s 6d per week, from which 12s was deducted for room and board, but she also got over-time payments. By the end of the war, girls at Gretna had a basic wage of 55s per week. Not surprisingly, there was some consternation among families who expected to be waited on and who suddenly found themselves faced with a serious staff problem, especially among the lower paid kitchen and scullery maids. At Annan, a few miles from Gretna, employers were offering six-month contracts of £12 to £16 for staff. But it was not just about money. The girls at Gretna had a degree of freedom in their lives that was denied to domestic servants. Their living conditions were also very different from the shared attic rooms of the domestic servants.

The township that grew up at Gretna was designed by Raymond Unwin, one of the pioneers of the garden city movement, having worked at both Letchworth and Hampstead Garden Suburb. There were hostels for unmarried girls and houses for families. The hostels held either 120 or 90 girls each. They had cook-housekeepers and maids who did all the cleaning. Each girl had a bed and storage space in a cubicle that could be closed off by a curtain. The food was good and one worker described it as being 'a lady's life in a way'. The one major complaint was that the wooden huts were never very warm. In winter when girls tried to mop the floor, the water often turned to ice before they had a chance to finish the job. Not everyone lived in the huts, and some girls moved into digs in nearby towns.

The girls who lived on site were still some distance from the works and were picked up at 6 a.m. for a twelve-hour shift and a sixty-

hour week. Not surprisingly they wanted to enjoy their time off
and make the most of their new freedom. Some went into town and
stayed out for the night. There was a very real sense that the authorities distrusted the girls' moral sense, and tried to regulate their spare
time as well as their working hours. The benevolent way they did
this at Gretna was to provide leisure facilities, though they tended at
first to be of the morally irreproachable and physically healthy variety – the YWCA and a gym. But it was clear that the girls wanted
rather more fun – many probably felt that the last thing they needed
after a hard-working twelve-hour shift was even more exercise. Even
so, there were many who, willingly or not, took part in hearty games,
including the then quite new activity for women, playing football. A
poem written at the time suggests that it was not always as popular as
the organisers might have thought:

Only one more football practice
Only one more train to catch
Only one more goal to score
Then we've won this football match.
When this rotten match is over
Oh! How happy I shall be
When I get my blouse and skirt on
No more footballing for me.[8]

It was clear that not everyone wanted to be morally or physically
improved, but just wanted to have fun and relax. So, in time, dances
were organised and a pub was opened on site. It inevitably attracted
scathing criticism from the righteous who listed all the horrors that
emanated from such an establishment – everything from crime and
domestic violence to alcoholism and syphilis. Yet the returns from
the Gretna Tavern showed that 70 per cent of the takings came from
food and more was spent on soft drinks than on beer. Basically, the
pub was a place where the girls could have a good time on their own
terms. As for the dire warnings of immorality and sexual diseases, a
government report produced at the end of the war showed a total of

just seventeen cases of venereal disease among the hundreds of thousands of women workers, and there were only 171 births recorded to unmarried mothers.

Many girls, however, still preferred to make their way to the nearest big town. There they were closely monitored by the newly formed women's police force, who were generally recruited from the ranks of middle-class women, and a number had formerly been suffragettes. They tended to be censorious, and concerned about what these girls might get up to while their husbands and sweethearts were away at the front. One of these new constables wrote about the girls as being 'wilful and pleasure loving' and 'wasting their time'. And they were in moral danger. To which the girls might very reasonably have replied that the vast majority of their time was spent on war work, and why shouldn't they have a bit of pleasure as well? Some factories, however, took a far sterner view. Supervisors could be high-handed. One refused to give permission for girls to go into town on a Saturday. Some went anyway and were promptly sacked. The result was a strike by the rest of the girls, and a group came and pelted the supervisor's house with plants torn up from her own garden. She resigned and the dispute was settled.

The munitions girls attracted a lot of interest and many of those who wrote about them seemed more interested in the moral question than in what they were actually doing. Mrs Ellis Chadwick was one of these, and offered this slightly unlikely version of meeting the girls for the first time:

> There came into view a pretty sight of daintily clad girls, all neat and tidy, coming from the direction of the works, but their healthy appearances suggested milkmaids … but on questioning the second group I found they were all munitions girls happy, bright and gay.[9]

Typically she felt that the work was good for the girls: 'the absence of tawdry jewellery, showy dresses and much befrizzed hair was very noticeable'. She found their northern accents had been 'softened and refined', but she clearly did not think they were looking towards an independent future. 'A girl who has had the advantage of doing her bit will be a better wife and mother.' Rebecca West, quoted earlier, was one of those who took the trouble to look a little more closely at what the girls actually did:

> One girl stands high on a platform against the wall, filling the cordite paste into one of the two great iron presses, and when she has finished with that she swings round the other one on a swivel with a fine, free gesture. The other girls stand round the table laying out the golden cords in graduated sizes from the thickness of rope to the thinness of macaroni, the clear khaki and scarlet of their dresses shining back from the wet floor in a perpetually changing pattern as they move quickly about their work. They look very young in their pretty, childish dresses and one thinks them good children for working so diligently. And it occurs to one as something incredible that they are now doing the last three hours of a twelve-hour shift.

Their 'pretty, childish dresses' were, in fact, not fashion statements, but a fire-resistant uniform. Only a few days before West's visit they had been sorely needed:

> There had been one of those incalculable happenings of which high explosives are so liable, an inflammatory mixture of air and acetone, with the cordite was ignited. Two huts were instantly gutted and the girls had to walk out through the flames. In spite of the uniform one girl lost her hand. These, of course, are the everyday dangers of the high-explosive factory.

West added the very just comment: 'It is a cold fact that they face more danger every day than any soldier on home defence has since the start of the war.' The incident she described was clearly very serious, but there were far worse in many other factories. At Silvertown, in London, an explosion killed 73 workers; at Faversham, 105 died. But the worst disaster was at Chilwell, Nottingham. This was one of Britain's most productive factories and it was said that the majority of the shells fired by the British during the Somme offensive came from there. Then in July 1918 there was a devastating explosion, in which an estimated 8 tons of TNT went up. The result was that 134 workers died and approximately 250 were injured. Lord Chetwynd, who had been responsible for setting up the factory, claimed it was due to sabotage and passed names to Scotland Yard. An enquiry was set up, but no report was ever published, so the cause remains a mystery. However, given the nature of the industry, it is perfectly possible that it was the result of a genuine accident, of the sort that was always possible where so many dangers were always and inevitably present. It is a macabre coincidence that this was the factory that had been chosen by Pathé to film the cheery girls at work.

Whatever the dangers involved in the work, and however some self-important commentators might try to belittle the girls, for most who reported on their achievements their efforts were heroic. A letter in *The Times* gave a telling account of their enthusiasm – and even overenthusiasm:

> There is apparently no limit to the work which Lancashire women can undertake. It ranges from designing to the 'bottling' of shells under heavy compressed air hammers. There is apparently no limit also to the eagerness of the women to get on with their work if one may judge by the notice which is posted in large type in one shell shop: – 'Warning. Anyone starting a machine before the bell will be instantly dismissed'. The girls, it was explained, were so anxious to get the utmost output that at the beginning of the shift or after the mid-day break they would sometimes start a machine cutting with steel before the main driving motor had reached sufficient speed to take the strain.[10]

The value of their work was aptly summed up by Sir Arthur Conan Doyle, writing in 1916: 'We can never beat Hindenberg until we beat Krupp, and that is what these khaki-clad girls of Moorside are going to do. Hats off to the women of Britain.'[11]

6

STEEL AND THE BIG GUNS

The development of artillery is so closely tied to developments in metallurgy that it is quite impossible to understand how guns developed without knowing something about the materials that were available for making them and the ways in which they could be worked. Modern gunnery really began with the change from cast-iron cannon lobbing out solid metal balls to guns firing shells. It all started early in the nineteenth century and the new artillery first saw action in the Crimean War of the 1850s. An improved type of gun had been developed that could fire for longer distances and with greater accuracy, thanks to the invention of the rifled barrel. Rifling consists of cutting a spiral groove inside the barrel. A flange at one end of the shell engages with the groove, so that as it travels the shell is made to spin. It is the spinning action that improves the trajectory. There was a problem, however, with rifling. Guns were still being made out of cast iron, which is brittle and was found to crack under the strain created by the shell travelling up the grooves. The big question was whether or not the iron masters could come up with an answer.

Iron masters had always had an important role to play in improving artillery. John Wilkinson, for example, back in the eighteenth century had been the first to devise machinery for accurately boring cannon.

But now there was a real problem. Iron comes in three main varieties: cast iron, wrought iron and steel. In the early days of the iron industry, the metal had been extracted from its ore by heating in a blast furnace using charcoal as a fuel. The air was blasted in to raise the temperature of the furnace to the point where it would melt the iron oxide, in the form of ores such as haematite, and the oxygen that was driven off would unite with the carbon of the charcoal to form carbon dioxide. The resulting molten iron that was then tapped off was very pure and is known as wrought iron, simply because it can be wrought – shaped by hammering. This is the iron of the blacksmith's forge. It is a metal that is very strong in tension, but which bends under compression.

One of the main disadvantages of the charcoal furnace was that it used a very large amount of a commodity that had a limited supply: timber. A lot of trees had to be chopped down to make enough charcoal just to keep one furnace going. The obvious answer would have been to turn to a much more abundant fuel: coal. The trouble was that the coal introduced far too many impurities into the iron, such as sulphur. Early in the eighteenth century Abraham Darby developed a new method using coke as a fuel: coal that has previously been heated, driving off the unwanted impurities. Limestone also had to be added, which united with the impurities in the ore to form slag that could be tapped off separately from the molten metal. It was highly successful, but now the iron that emerged had a comparatively high carbon content that gave it very different characteristics from wrought iron. It was, by contrast, weak in tension and strong in compression, but it was ideal for casting – hence cast iron. Because the coke furnace was far better in so many ways than the old charcoal furnace, the next step was to develop a method of turning some of the cast iron into wrought iron. This was achieved by Henry Cort at his forge near Portsmouth in 1784. He heated cast iron in a reverbatory furnace, one in which the metal never comes into direct contact with the fuel, in a process known as puddling. So now there were two very different forms of iron available, each of which had its own characteristics and that could be worked in different ways. The problem of making efficient gun barrels, however, still had to be solved.

There was a material that was ideal, the third common form of iron – steel. It is characterised by having a carbon content part way between that of cast and wrought iron, and having some of the characteristics of both, strong in both compression and tension. It would have been ideal for manufacturing guns, as it would be strong enough to withstand the explosive forces of firing, and hard yet malleable enough for the grooves needed for rifling to be cut without the risk of fracture. But steel manufacture was difficult, labour intensive and expensive. In the 1850s Britain was the biggest producer of iron in the world, turning out 3.5 million tons, but little more than 50,000 tons of steel. It was insufficient for any sort of major manufacturing industry, so if guns were to be improved someone had to work out how to do that with the materials that were readily available. The first man to find the answer was William Armstrong. His first hugely profitable engineering venture came when he began developing cranes using hydraulic power, which he manufactured at a factory at Elswick on the Tyne, above Newcastle. His interest in armaments began during the Crimean War when he devised a type of submarine mine for the Admiralty. It was never used but it did bring another problem to his attention. The 18-pounder guns being used in the war were so heavy – with the carriage and limber weighing in at a hefty 3 tons – that the army often found it impossible to move them. Armstrong felt he could do better and began to develop a lighter field gun.

He knew that greater accuracy could be achieved with rifling, but that it needed a hard steel to withstand the forces exerted during firing. But it only needed to be a thin steel tube. The main barrel that encased it used wrought iron, which was wound into a spiral that was heated and hammered together to form a solid tube, with a second tube welded above that. All had to be carefully machined to fit smoothly, and the rifling presented special difficulties. It was said that Armstrong stayed in the factory all night to ensure that the process went smoothly. This was a breech-loaded gun, unlike the older cannon, where the projectile was dropped in from the end of the barrel, and was designed to fire shells. It was tested at Shoeburyness against an unrifled gun of the same calibre: the Armstrong gun was twice as accurate over 2 miles as the other was over just 1 mile.

The Woolwich Arsenal proved incapable of making the guns, so Armstrong began manufacturing them himself at Elswick, as the Elswick Ordnance Company. In 1868 they went into partnership with the warship builder Charles Mitchell & Co., whose yards lay on the Tyne, 5 miles downriver from Elswick. Improvements to navigation on the Tyne gave Armstrong the chance to boost his business in naval gunnery, if he could get the battleships to use the river to reach his works. He was granted permission to remove the old stone bridge that blocked his way and replace it with a new hydraulic swing bridge made, of course, by Armstrong. It is still there, with its original hydraulic machinery still doing the job. It was opened in 1876 and was a suitably grand advertisement for Armstrong and all his works. The Italian *Europa*, the largest warship of the day, steamed up the Tyne past the new bridge, to Elswick, where the largest hydraulic lifting gear ever built lifted the largest gun ever built on board. Armstrong had by now established the value of the breech-loading rifled gun, firing shells, though there were problems with the breech-loading mechanism at first. The Elswick Ordnance Company was to be one of the major suppliers of guns throughout the First World War.

Armstrong was by no means the only inventive engineer showing an interest in improving guns and artillery. Joseph Whitworth had begun his working life as a mechanic in the textile industry, but his life changed when he managed to get a job with one of the great engineers of the day, Henry Maudslay. His talents were recognised and his first great achievement came when he designed and built a tool for planing the surfaces of steam engine valves to very fine tolerances. He was concerned with accuracy and reproducibility and is best known for regulating the manufacture of screws, with a thread that was always at the same angle of 55° and an average pitch for different diameters. The system of standardisation was named after him.

It was this reputation for working with great accuracy that led the Board of Ordnance to ask Whitworth to design machinery for manufacturing a rifled musket during the Crimean War. Whitworth declined on the grounds that he needed to know a lot more before he could begin, such as which was the best bore and what form the rifling should take. He came up with a rifle of .45in bore, which was tested against the standard weapon produced by the official Royal Small Arms Factory at Enfield. In the trial, the Whitworth gun 'excelled the Enfield to a degree which hardly leaves room for comparison'.[1] The War Office declined to take it on the grounds that it was too small, though a later committee recommended .45in as the ideal bore for a military weapon. Whitworth went on to devise a cannon, on a slightly different principle to that of Armstrong's, but this again was rejected by the War Office. It did not deter Whitworth from making further improvements, but there is no doubt that the mandarins of Whitehall were always more likely to hold back improvement rather than encourage it. It was a state of affairs that was all too familiar to pioneering engineers. The great Isambard Brunel had designed a new type of gunboat during the Crimean War, but was horrified to find that his ideas had been sent to the Admiralty:

> You assume that something has been done or is doing in the matter which I spoke to you about last month – did you not know that it has been brought within the withering influence of the Admiralty and that (of course) therefore, the curtain has dropped upon it and nothing had resulted? It would exercise the intellects of our acutest philosophers to investigate and discover the powerful agent which acts upon all matters brought within the range of the mere atmosphere of this department … they have an unlimited supply of some *negative* principle which seems to absorb and eliminate everything that approaches them.[2]

The negative principle seemed just as strong in the lead-up to the First World War, as we shall see over and over again. In the meantime, the whole question of how best to make guns was given new impetus by a major shift in technology.

The first breakthrough towards the manufacture of steel in large quantities was due to experiments carried out by William Kelly in America, and although he received a patent for his process he went bankrupt before he could profit from it. He discovered that if pig iron – another name for cast iron – was heated to a high temperature and then had air blown through it, the temperature could be raised as the carbon itself acted as a fuel. A similar idea was being pursued at the same time in Britain by Henry Bessemer, who was to have rather more commercial success. What he had not realised was that he had been fortunate in doing his first experiments with pig iron that was free from phosphorus – which was not true of most pig iron produced from British ores. His first efforts were not entirely successful: the steel was brittle and full of blowholes. Part of the answer was found by introducing spiegeleisen, a manganese and iron alloy that got rid of the blowholes, and it could also be used to regulate the carbon content. In Sweden it was discovered that the best results were obtained using iron from the local Dannemora ores that were very pure and free from phosphorus. The end result of all these experiments was the Bessemer converter. The whole converter was pivoted, which enabled the molten metal to be poured in and out without heat loss. When in the vertical position, with the air blast blowing through, it produced an astonishing pyrotechnic display, as sparks hurled out from the open top of the converter, like an industrial volcano.

An alternative method of steel production was invented at much the same time as the Bessemer converter. Frederick Siemens developed an open-hearth furnace. As the name suggests, the pig iron was heated in a shallow oblong hearth, the heat in later versions being supplied by gas, which brought the metal up to the very high temperature of 1,650 °C. Cheap scrap iron could be added to the pure pig iron, which made it a very economical and efficient system. Together, the two new systems ensured that large quantities of high-grade steel could now be produced at a reasonable cost.

This was good news for armament manufacturers, who could do away with the difficult job of using wrought iron as an outer casing for the steel tube in large guns. Whitworth was encouraged into fresh experiments. He knew that guns made of hard steel were likely to explode when they became worn, whereas ductile steel merely became deformed. The trouble was that ductile steel tended to have its own problem – when cast into ingots there was a honeycomb effect caused by air bubbles. He solved this by subjecting the steel to high pressure using hydraulic presses. It is a little ironic that Armstrong's greatest rival made his major breakthrough using hydraulics – the system that had first made Armstrong's own fortune. Even more ironically, in 1897, ten years after Whitworth's death, the two great rival arms manufacturers were united to create Armstrong Whitworth, whose work was to prove essential throughout the Great War.

This rather lengthy historical preamble highlights various factors that were vital to the work of the gun makers throughout the war. The first lesson was that it was not always possible to rely on the government and its civil servants being good judges of what the country needed. The second is that the technology of gun making had developed hand-in-hand with advances in metallurgy and the two were inseparable. Both the Bessemer and Siemens processes were ultimately dependent on the quality of the raw materials fed into their fiery hearts. Manufacturers at least had the consolation of knowing that, when Lloyd George took over responsibility for armaments, they were dealing with a man and a department that understood something of the world of business and was imbued with a real sense of urgency. Keeping the furnaces going, however, was to prove more problematic.

Britain had become increasingly reliant on countries such as Sweden and Spain for its high-quality iron that was the basis of all the steel processes. As the demand for steel went up so the supplies from overseas went down, sometimes quite literally, due to the action of German submarines. The change had to be made from the rich ores from overseas to what were often poorer quality ores available in Britain. A special Iron and Steel Production Department was set up, as part of the Ministry of Munitions, and Sir John Hunter was put in charge. The task was daunting:

[It involved] such sweeping changes in plant, supplies, inland transport, labour etc., that it could only have been carried out with difficulty in peace time. Under war conditions it was evident that the problems would receive the most skilful handling by a carefully organised department ... It is a remarkable tribute to the latent organising power of the nation that, under the adverse conditions of a great war, it should have been possible to raise the steel production of the country to the highest point it has ever reached.[3]

Steel was essential to the whole armaments industry, as well as others, such as shipbuilding. To manufacture it required ore, special types of sand for casting, coal suitable for turning into coke for the furnaces and other materials 'that had been allowed to lie dormant'.

Early in 1916 it was decided that it would be essential to increase the supply of pig iron – and that would require new supplies of raw materials. It had been hoped that France, for example, might provide some ore, but the French had enough difficulty meeting the demands of their own industry and had no inclination to let any of the valuable commodity out of the country – even to an ally. New ironstone mines and limestone quarries were opened up, with the help of German prisoners of war. By the end of the year there were 1,500 of them at work. Some of these were non-combatants, who were known as 'interned aliens', in other words, Germans who happened to be in Britain at the start of the war, many of whom had been in the country, living and working quite happily, for many years. They may have resented being treated as suspicious aliens, but they worked well and were paid on reasonable piece rates. The rest were the more familiar captured servicemen. They were not exactly an ideal workforce, since they could hardly be expected to show any great enthusiasm for providing the raw materials that would end up being used to kill their former comrades. Even if they had been willing, strictly enforced rules meant that not only did they get paid a pittance, but they could only be fed prison rations, which were acceptable in a camp, but totally inadequate for a life of hard manual labour. Prisoner labour made a difference, but still failed to make up the full losses in imported materials.

Other workers were brought in. Welsh slate workers were described by a contemporary as of 'inferior physique', and when they found that they could not earn enough from their labours soon went home again. Men brought in from the Cornish china clay industry fared a good deal better. The situation was improved by the introduction of mechanisation at some of the opencast iron ore mines. Steam diggers were brought in and light railways laid. Trucks were commandeered from wherever they could be obtained, and harassed officials tried to shuffle rolling stock around to where it was most needed. It was inevitable that mistakes were made: for example, sites where loading was only possible if trucks had low sides got ones with high sides, and vice versa.

The various schemes that were tried and the many different type of worker employed did increase production of iron ore, but there was also the problem of quality as well as quantity. Many old sites were investigated, such as the Forest of Dean, where iron ore had been mined since at least Roman times, and Ireland, but they proved impractical for modern use. New developments were made possible in the Midlands and Cleveland with the opening up of opencast mines, using the latest machinery. Another new mine opened in Oxfordshire, to the north-west of Banbury, was so important that a special branch line was built to take the raw material to the main Great Western Railway line for shipment direct to the furnaces of South Wales. It had a very special importance because many of the Welsh iron and steel works had become dependent on Spanish haematite, the iron ore that gets its name from its blood-red colour. The most important area for haematite mining in Britain was Cumberland, where 5,000 were employed in mines by 1918, and where the ore went directly to local blast furnaces. A pamphlet written shortly before the start of the war was to prove prophetic:

> It will be the fault of those most closely interested if the manufacture of pure Bessemer Steel does not, in the long run, benefit the district. We produce no inferior class of iron, and can therefore be trusted not to adulterate … The ore beds of the district are far from being exhausted, and may stand us in good stead, when those totally dependent on Spain fall short of supplies.[4]

The greatest of these mines was Hodbarrow on the Cumbrian coast near Millom. It was first developed in the 1840s and remained open until 1968, during which time some 25 million tons of ore was extracted. It was, in fact, so close to the sea that elaborate defences had to be erected to keep out the water at high tides, including a vast barrier made out of furnace slag. The system of working the mines traditionally depended on 'companies' of miners, groups of up to twelve men who made an agreement with the management based on payment of an agreed price for the ore. The more they extracted, the better they were paid, though there was a fallback position. Sometimes the work proved more difficult than expected or there were unexpected hold-ups, in which case management would make a supplementary payment. Terms were regularly set on a fortnightly basis. The companies consisted of the actual miners and the 'trailers', usually boys or young men who moved the ore from the working face to the bottom of the shaft for hauling to the surface. This worked well in peacetime. There was an incentive to work hard and the pay went up as the value of ore increased. It was similar in many ways to the systems in use in the tin and copper mines of south-west England. It produced a very independent-minded workforce, who had to rely on their own knowledge and judgement when negotiating the price for their work, based in good measure on how they estimated the value of the ore. In wartime things were very different. The price of ore was no longer fixed by the market but by the government: it remained static but the cost of living was rising all the time. The old Conciliation Board no longer dealt with the problem, which was now passed to the ministry in London, who worked to very different rules and guidelines. The union was soon pressing for better conditions.

The ministry's response was to propose bringing extra miners into Cumberland. The Cumberland Miners' Association sent a note to the proprietors demanding that no outsiders should be employed until all those already working in the mine, who were over 21 and had three years' practical experience, were made up to full miners. At the same time, they put in a claim for an increase in the minimum wage. They gave a fortnight's notice that if their demands were not met they would go on strike. In June 1917 the government took over the running of the mine and in August the men came out on strike. According to the deal agreed with Lloyd George there should have been no strikes during the war years, so what went wrong? The obvious first cause was that the men saw a steady decline in their living standards. A contributing factor was that they now had to deal not with a management that knew the area and understood the problem but with men from Whitehall who did neither. In the event, negotiations resulted in an increase in the minimum wage and a new bonus scheme. Outsiders were still encouraged to come to Cumberland, and a number of Scottish miners came south, though few stayed for very long.

The war industries were demanding ever greater quantities of steel, but it was never just a question of supplying whatever steel happened to be available or easy to make: it had to be the right kind of steel for the job. Some 30 per cent of all the steel manufactured was used in shells, since the army had an almost insatiable appetite for ammunition. Fortunately, some suitable shell steel could still be imported from the United States. Much of it arrived by sea in Liverpool, where it was taken via the Manchester Ship Canal to a new factory at Trafford Park. The site occupied 45 acres and had 8 miles of internal railway lines. In full production it was swallowing 14,000 tons of steel per week and turning it into 150,000 shells. And the demand kept changing as new industries, such as aircraft manufacturing, found that they needed supplies of special alloy steels. Technical staff were sent to visit steel manufacturers who had been used to providing one sort of steel in order to see how they could meet the different demands of war and provide specialist steels, such as that required for armaments and munitions. But given a huge demand that kept growing throughout the war years, it was inevitable that arms manufacturers and others sometimes just had to make use of what was actually available as opposed to what was ideally required. Standards had to be lowered and steels with higher percentages of both phosphorus and sulphur had to be accepted.

The whole industry was strictly controlled. Before the war, British steel manufacturers had enjoyed a healthy export trade. That was now severely curtailed and only steel that had been allowed under special licence was permitted to be sent abroad. The government also fixed prices, and steel companies found it difficult to maintain their former profitability. There were, however, compensations. They were allowed to modernise, to buy new plant at pre-war prices with government aid, and that plant would still be there for them when peace finally arrived. Between 1916 and 1918, a total of twenty-two new blast furnaces had been built and 166 steel furnaces, mostly now open hearth. This should all have led to greatly improved production, but there was still another problem to overcome. In the early years of the war many foundry workers had volunteered and when conscription came in the iron workers were not given exemption. Just when iron and steel were in greatest demand many furnaces had to be closed down for want of anyone to work them. The industry estimated that it was short some 600 skilled operatives, and pleas for them to be released from the army to carry out essential war work at home fell on deaf War Office ears. The argument that a man was better employed helping to make thousands of guns than he would be firing just one was ignored. Somehow, the supply of iron and steel was maintained to the end, but at times it seemed like a very close thing.

The manufacture of the implements of war require many different types of processes to be used. One of the oldest is casting. The principle is simple. In its earliest form, the process started by making a pattern of the finished article out of wood. This was a highly skilled job. I have a pattern for a 9in-diameter cog that sits on the windowsill of my study. It has a solid circular core and thirteen teeth, each of which has been carefully shaped and set into the central core with a neat mortise and tenon joint. It is a piece of workmanship that any skilled carpenter would be happy to claim as his own. This would have been put in a casting box and packed round with sand, not just any old sand but a very special variety. A 1930s manual lists eight different types of sand that were then in regular use.[5] There would be other ingredients mixed in, such as coal dust that helps to prevent overheating. The pattern was then removed, leaving its shape behind as a hollow in the sand. Molten metal was then poured in and would take the shape of the original pattern. In the eighteenth century, cannon would have been cast in the solid in this way and then bored out by drill. Hollow objects can also be cast, by using a core that remains in place during the casting process. The final object would need further machining for an accurate finish. This is a very simplified account, but the general system has scarcely changed, only become more sophisticated.

When hot metal is not cast in a complex shape it is simply allowed to form ingots or billets, oblong blocks. Treating these can involve some of the most imposing examples of heavy engineering. The other very ancient method of working metal is in the forge, seen at its simplest with the blacksmith and his anvil, hammering metal into shape. Early mechanisation involved the use of tilt hammers, origi-nally powered by a waterwheel. In its basic form, a projection on a rotating wheel engaged with one end of the hammer so that the head was lifted. As the wheel turned on, the projection was cleared and the hammer's head dropped down on the anvil under gravity. A single wheel could be used to turn a number of hammers. Problems arose when it came to forging very large hunks of metal, simply because there was a limit to how high the head could be raised. This arose when Isambard Brunel wanted an enormous crankshaft for his new proposed steamer the *Great Britain* in 1839. The man who found the answer was the engineer James Nasmyth, who promptly invented a steam hammer. Steam pressure was used to raise a heavy metal block running within a guiding metal frame. Once the steam was cut off by a valve the metal block dropped. It was later improved by using steam pressure on the downward stroke as well to increase the power of the hammer. The steam hammer was in regular use in engineering firms throughout the early years of the twentieth century. Perhaps the most remarkable thing about this device is just how short a time there was between Nasmyth being sent the problem by Francis Humphreys, who was designing the engine for Brunel, and coming up with the solution. Here is Nasmyth's own description:

I got out my 'Scheme Book', on the pages of which I generally *thought out*, with the aid of pen and pencil, such mechanical adaptations as

I had conceived in my mind, and was thereby enabled to render them visible. I then rapidly sketched out my Steam Hammer, having it all clearly before me in my mind's eye. In little more than half an hour, after receiving Mr. Humphries' letter narrating an unlooked for difficulty, I had the whole contrivance in all its executant details, before me in a page of the Scheme Book.[6]

That page still exists and he was not exaggerating: the sketch is exactly what was manufactured. That is engineering genius. The men who operated these giant hammers were highly skilled. By controlling the action of the valves they could manage every movement of the hammer with extraordinary accuracy. A famous demonstration of skill involved putting an egg on the anvil, then bringing down the hammer so that it came to rest touching the shell without breaking it. One can see why employers were anxious to keep such men from joining the cannon fodder on the Western Front.

That was not the only way of working with big steel billets – they could also be hot-rolled into sheets of whatever thickness was required, from thin plates for boiler making to thicker armour plates. The method was exactly what the name suggests. The ingots were brought to white heat then passed through a series of rollers, first through one, then back in the opposite direction through the next. It was essential that the work was carried out quickly before the metal had a chance to cool and became unworkable. It was a job that required a very special sort of powerful engine, and just such engines were supplied to Cammell, one of the leading manufacturers of armour plating in Sheffield. The engine began work in 1905 and was still in use in the 1970s, but for an industry that had not even been dreamed of when it was first started up: it made protective shields for nuclear power stations. At the end of its working life it found a home in the Sheffield industrial museum on Kelham Island. It is a truly remarkable machine, an immense steam engine that stands 28ft high and weighs a massive 426 tons. It has three cylinders, each 41in in diameter and uses steam at the high pressure of 160lb per square inch (psi) to generate 12,000hp. Perhaps the most remarkable thing about this engine is that it is reversible: it can stop, then restart turning in the opposite direction in just two seconds. This was essential to ensure that the metal could pass from one set of rollers turning in one direction, and then back through the next set turning the opposite way, as quickly as possible (it is regularly demonstrated at the museum, and is breathtaking: the sight of it in motion even reduced my busily chatting young grandson to silent astonishment). The work of the rolling mills was physically demanding, not just because of the heavy labour involved in handling great weights of metal, but also from the intense heat that was an always-present factor.

The armament industry was equipped with the right machines and the appropriate materials that were needed for the war, but it was always a struggle to keep output equal to the ever-growing demand. One of the most pressing problems was making good the loss of valuable imported materials, a situation that was not helped by the Admiralty's long-term resistance to providing adequate protection to merchant shipping. There was also the problem of finding sufficient skilled labour: a problem that was constant throughout the armaments industry.

7

SMALL ARMS

The development of the small arms industry has a crucial place in industrial history. It introduced the world to the idea of the manufacture of interchangeable parts, the basis for all modern mass-production methods. It was Eli Whitney, the inventor of the cotton gin, who came up with the idea of mass-producing standardised weapons in a factory. Previously a gun had been made as a one-off item and no two were exactly the same, so that if, for example, a part was damaged you couldn't simply take a replacement out of store, but had to make a new one to measure – or throw the old gun away. What Whitney proposed was using machines to make the individual components, so that each one manufactured would have exactly the same dimensions as the next: every trigger would be exactly the same as every other trigger and so on. Assembling them into the finished gun was the final stage in the process. In 1812 he offered to make 15,000 muskets. In his application to the US Government, he wrote that he was working on 'a plan which is unknown in Europe' and 'the great leading object of which is to substitute correct and effective operations of machinery for that skill of the artist which is acquired only by long practice and experience'.[1] The authorities in Washington were unconvinced until Whitney arrived to give a demonstration. He brought with him the parts of ten muskets, scattered them on a table and then indiscriminately picked up the different parts and assembled ten identical muskets. It was enough to convince the sceptics. The basic idea was developed further by Samuel Colt in making his famous revolver, and what became known as the 'American system' soon attracted interest in Britain.

In 1853 James Nasmyth was appointed to the Small Arms Committee that had been given the job of completely reorganising the Royal Small Arms Factory (RSAF) at Enfield. Colt had already established a small factory in London, but the committee accepted an invitation to visit the United States factory at Springfield. They came back full of enthusiasm for the American system, as Nasmyth explained:

> The committee immediately proceeded with the entire remodelling of the Small Arms Factory at Enfield. The workshops were equipped with a complete series of special machine tools obtained from the Springfield factory. The United States Government also permitted some of their best and most experienced workers and superintendents to take service under the British Government.[2]

Joseph Whitworth, who also worked on the committee with Nasmyth, had his own explanation of why new ideas were suddenly appearing from across the Atlantic, rather than being developed in Britain:

> The labouring classes [in America] are comparatively few in number, but this is counterbalanced by, and indeed may be regarded as one of the chief causes of, the eagerness with which they call in the aid of machinery … wherever it can be introduced, it is universally and willingly resorted to.[3]

The British at least showed that they were equally willing to turn to new methods and even improve on them. The Enfield factory was reorganised with new machine tools and when fully operational was expected to be able to turn out 2,000 rifles per week, the manufacture of each one of which required 700 separate operations.

Enfield continued to take advantage of new methods and tools being developed in America. Robbins & Lawrence had introduced a number of new machine tools for many tasks, including barrel drilling and rifling. When they exhibited in London in 1851 they sold a number of machines to Enfield.

The armament industry depended on the accuracy of its machine tools. Just taking one apparently simple part of the gun, the barrel, what can seem on first glance as just a plain tube has to be machined to very fine tolerances. The first task is boring out the barrel from the solid. The hole has to be straight, so most gun barrels produced during the war years, instead of trying to force a rotating drill bit down to create a hole (that was always liable to judder) used a stationary bit and rotated the barrel at high speed, anything up to 5,000 revolutions per minute. The bit itself was mounted on a long steel tube with a groove down the side. Coolant oil was forced down the groove at high pressure, which simultaneously maintained a low temperature and cleared away the swarf, the metal shavings. The barrel was not drilled to the exact bore. The next process was reaming to shave off the final few millimetres of metal. This time, the oil-cooled drill bit was moved inside the barrel. The next stage would be to rifle the barrel. The most common tool used was the sine bar rifler. In this, a cutter box is pulled through and as it moves it is rotated to impart the twist to the rifling. Only about a ten thousandth of an inch of metal would be removed at each pass, so the process had to be repeated a number of times until the required depth of groove was reached. This was precision engineering at the very limit of the available technology.

One man whose name was to be famously associated with that of Enfield was James P. Lee. He came originally from Scotland, but his family emigrated to Canada when he was just 5 years old. As a gun maker he introduced two important innovations in 1879, when he designed a .303 calibre rifle with a spring-loaded magazine that held five cartridges and a simple bolt action that greatly improved the speed and efficiency of loading and firing. In 1888 the British Army took on the Mk 1 rifle, but when rifles were built that used cordite instead of gunpowder as a propellant, it was found to cause overheating and excessive wear. This time the problem was solved not in America but in Britain, at the Small Arms Factory and the redesigned model was produced in 1895. It was the first Lee-Enfield rifle. Further improvements were made to the weapon, including shortening the length of the barrel so that it could be used by both infantry and cavalry. This was the Short Lee-Enfield, first introduced in 1902, which was to be the standard infantry weapon throughout the First World War and for a long time after. It was still standard issue in the Second World War and a satisfactory replacement was only introduced in 1957. It has been estimated that altogether some 17 million of these rifles were manufactured.

In its final version it retained the bolt action but had a magazine that held ten rounds of ammunition. It was comparatively light at just under 9lb (though anyone who has had to march long distances with one on their shoulder probably wouldn't think so) and was an effective weapon, with a range of well over 0.25 miles. It will be familiar to anyone who has ever seen film or photographs of the army during either of the World Wars. However, although it was standard issue for the infantry, the generals at the start of the First World War still hung on to the old idea of gallantly charging cavalry. Lt Gen. Sir John French made the official view quite clear shortly before hostilities began: 'It would be a fatal mistake to permit the Cavalry to regard the rifle as their principal weapon. All spirit and élan would go with this new departure, and if engaged in a European war such an organisation would be fatal.' This was the man who would shortly become the commander-in-chief of the British Expeditionary Force of 1914.

One major improvement in small arms performance did not originate in America. The muzzle-loaded gun had given way to the breech-loaded version early in the nineteenth century, with the detonator, propellant and the bullet contained in a single paper cartridge. The very obvious problem was that if the cartridge got wet it no longer worked. E.M. Boxer, who worked in the laboratory associated with Woolwich Arsenal, developed a metal cartridge. The base was made of iron and the walls of coiled brass wire, with the bullet sealing the nose. It was not very successful, mainly because the coiling caused it to jam. It was obvious, however, that metal was very much better than paper, and a more appropriate design soon followed.

The inventor of what became the standard brass cartridge started his working life in a very different environment. George Kynoch was born in Scotland, had a limited education and started off as a bank clerk. He was ambitious and moved to Birmingham for a better job in a bigger bank. Birmingham had for a long time been famous – and at times infamous – for gun making. In the eighteenth century there was a very profitable line in making muskets for the slave trade. They were exchanged with local chiefs for the slaves, but it was as well for the chiefs if they never tried to fire them. They were so badly made that they were more liable to blow up in the chief's face than they were to hit the intended target. The scandal led reputable makers to press for the creation of the Gun Barrel Proof House to guarantee the quality of all guns made in the area. It is still there and still doing the same job, using essentially the same method. Each gun would be rated to show the recommended explosive charge for safe use. The proof house would then overcharge and fire it. If everything worked satisfactorily it had passed the test: if it blew up no one could argue with the result afterwards. So when Kynoch arrived in Birmingham the gun trade was sound and well regulated. It looked more interesting and exciting than filling in ledgers in a bank.

He joined a company making ammunition – and was undeterred when an explosion at the works killed nineteen of the seventy employees. By 1868 he had set up on his own and in the same year he patented his version of the brass cartridge. It was so successful that cartridges of this type were still being made using virtually the same technology and methods in 1914. The process starts by punching a disc out of a brass strip, usually rather less than ⅛in thick, and forming it into a shallow cup. It is then heated to soften the metal and pickled to remove any scale. The cup is then worked on by a succession of punches and dies, each of slightly smaller diameter than the last, so that it is gradually drawn out into a cylinder, the process usually being repeated four times altogether.

The reorganisation of the RSAF to produce the Short Lee-Enfield caused real hardship for the workforce.[4] For many months, while old machines were being adapted and new ones installed, most of the men were put on part-time working. The fact that the Boer War had ended and demand for weaponry was also dropping off only added to the problem. Management did not help raise morale. For example, whereas previously if a man was told not to come in on a Thursday, he would get his pay that evening, now everyone had to turn up at the factory on a Saturday to collect their money. There were over 2,000 working at RSAF at the start of the twentieth century, but many were earning £1 per week or even less, and the War Office were looking to cut the workforce by at least 400. It all had a huge impact on the area: families were reduced to poverty and many local shops went out of business, simply because there was so little money around. There was large-scale unemployment and those in work were on little better than starvation wages.

In 1905 Balfour, the prime minister, set up a committee to look into the work of government factories, which included ordnance factories. The report published in 1907 recommended that the workforce at Enfield should be between 1,900 and 2,000, with a weekly wage bill not to exceed £4,000. It also recommended that government ordnance factories should not have more than one-third of the government orders, and that the rest should go to private companies: privatisation was not a twenty-first-century invention. The ordnance factories argued that as they had invested in a great deal of modernisation and had installed expensive machinery, they should be permitted to make the best use of it by producing other items besides armaments. They might, for example, take a share in the newly developing automobile industry. This was rejected by the government as a totally unacceptable challenge to free enterprise. Private companies could compete for armaments orders with government factories; the RSAF could not compete for other work carried out by private arms manufacturers. They were not the only government factory to suffer: the nearby Waltham Abbey gunpowder factory also dismissed 400 of their workers.

The privatisation policy soon began to show results. The Ordnance Factory at Sparkbrook in Birmingham was closed down and sold off to the Birmingham Small Arms Company (BSA), who were guaranteed a share in the manufacture of the Lee-Enfield. At Enfield itself things got no better for the workers. Older men were either fired or moved on to what was known as the 'labour gang' at reduced wages. A new system for drilling rifle barrels was introduced and the barrel setters, who had been among the more highly paid of the skilled workers, found their pay reduced from £2 per week to 26s per week. As late as May 1914, the government was announcing that there would be no pay rises – no one had had a wage increase for the past twelve years – and that they were expecting to make more redundancies and reduce output. There were widespread protests, but they had no effect. What makes it so remarkable is that the British who had failed to get an arms limitation treaty with Germany during 1910–11 was well aware that German armaments manufacture was going ahead at great speed, with what was probably the most innovative armaments company of the day, Krupp of Essen, selling 50 per cent of its output to the German Army. By May it must have seemed to anyone studying the international situation that war was very likely if not inevitable and that when it came it would be fought with twentieth-century technology. It is indicative of official thinking in the British Army that one department at RSAF that was kept moderately busy preparing for any future conflict was the one making swords for the cavalry.

With the declaration of war everything changed. Instead of being put on short time, men were being put on twelve-hour days and thirteen-day fortnights with substantial overtime to be earned. Unsurprisingly, army recruitment in the Enfield area was slow: men hoped to be taken on at the arms factory where they could earn good money rather than join up. Suddenly families had money to spare: bookmakers' runners did a brisk trade collecting bets and betting slips, and the four local pubs near the works were allowed to remain open until midnight, except on Sundays when they closed at midday (to supply the men on shift work). But, as elsewhere in the country, attitudes towards drinking were changing: anyone found drunk got a heavy fine. Then the authorities decided that more drastic action was needed. Instead of fining drunks, they introduced new regulations to try and prevent anyone getting drinks in the first place. In December 1915 the men coming out at 11 p.m. for their meal break found all the pubs were closed. The situation got dangerous, as furious workers found there was nowhere they could get a meal, let alone a pint. The superintendent in charge was forced to extend the usual break to two hours to allow the men who could get home to do so and to provide time for the factory dining hall to organise food for the rest. Many of those who went home decided not to bother to return that night: the measure designed to increase productivity had resulted in a huge loss of working hours. A compromise was reached that allowed the pubs to open from 11 p.m. to midnight to supply food, but not alcohol. Sunday opening was restricted to two hours from 1 p.m. By February 1916 all four pubs had been taken over by the government and two of them turned into canteens.

Now instead of making redundancies RSAF began recruiting, but refused to take men between the age of 19 and 35, who were expected to join the armed forces. Hundreds more applied than could be taken on. From being a workplace where the men struggled for a living wage, it was now somewhere that promised something far better. In 1915 the minimum rate for labourers was 6*d* per hour for a forty-eight-hour week, but they were paid time and a quarter for the first two hours overtime, then time and a half. As an eighty-two-hour week was now accepted as normal, a man would earn at least £2 11*s* per week, and if he worked Sundays he got even more, for that was on double pay. Skilled men did even better. The workers who had been struggling to live were now the subject of indignant letters to *The Times* claiming that they were being grossly overpaid.

The good news did not last. The most highly skilled workers found their expertise was not being recognised in their pay levels, with the Enfield engineers who had once been the highest paid in the region now falling behind others doing similar work elsewhere. The Amalgamated Society of Engineers (ASE) called several meetings that resulted in a demand for an increase of 10*s*: all they got was 3s. In May 1917, in spite of anti-strike agreements, 600 Enfield engineers walked out. The strike was opposed by the majority in the factory and it was short-lived. It was indicative of the problems caused by the wartime agreements. Colonel Fisher, the Enfield superintendent, pointed out that wages had increased greatly at RSAF with a general increase of 50 per cent for all workers, and some earning twice their pre-war wages thanks to the long hours and overtime, which was true. The ASE pointed out that the rise was illusory, since thanks to inflation, £1 now only bought half what it had done before the war. A fair assessment might be that workers at RSAF were better off in so far as they were constantly working full time, but the financial rewards never did more than keep step with rapidly rising prices. Yet in spite of the discontent, the ordnance factories served the country well.

One of the results of the influx of new workers was a desperate shortage of housing in the area. The problem was eased by building huts, similar to those provided for munitions workers at Gretna Green, for which men paid 17s 6d per week. The facilities were always overstretched: the kitchens could scarcely provide all the food needed, and the dining halls overflowed at meal times, so that men ate their food wherever they could find anywhere to perch, whether standing in a corridor or sitting on the stairs. Some help was provided by middle-class women from the town, who set up their own refreshment service. The housing shortage resulted in many having to travel long distances to get to work, but local transport proved hopelessly inadequate, mostly due to inefficient organisation. The tram company was working to outdated timetables, providing vehicles to places that no one wanted to visit, while the factory workers queued for the few trams that were going where most people needed to be. There was a train service to and from Liverpool Street Station, but the train times were not well co-ordinated with the working hours at RSAF and, in the early morning, men were left hanging around waiting for their shifts to start.

As in the munitions industry, women were soon being employed alongside the men, and the need for extra hands became acute once conscription was finally introduced in January 1916. At first there was considerable discord over just how many eligible young men were being kept on at RSAF and in the gunpowder factory at Waltham Abbey: it was said there were as many as 2,000 at Enfield alone. In the event, 395 young men left Enfield for the forces and 516 went from Waltham Abbey. A lot were kept on, simply because they were considered to have skills that could not easily be replaced, but in the fevered atmosphere of Britain in the war years there was intense pressure on them to be sent to the front. By the end of 1916 almost 1,000 women had taken up jobs at Enfield. Younger boys, under 18, were also taken on and by 1917 there was a total workforce of nearly 10,000, of which 15 per cent were women and 10 per cent were boys.

It was not only the human element that changed at Enfield during the war years. An immense amount of new work was carried out to improve efficiency. The factory no longer relied on its own generators for electricity – it was connected to the main supply from the power station at Brimsdown. Railway sidings were built in 1915 that proved of enormous value, with more than seventy trucks per day bringing in essential materials, some of which were forwarded by barge down the Lea Navigation to the gunpowder factory. The Enfield factory itself was extended and new machinery bought to ensure a steady supply of weapons. Nevertheless, problems ensued and one department nearly came to a halt: a new timber mill had been built for the manufacture of gunstocks, which were turned out at the rate of 30,000 per week, and though the machinery was more than adequate, there was a problem with supplying the walnut that was used. European supplies were cut off and most was imported from America, but the ships were under threat from the submarine campaign. Britain was scoured to find anyone holding any reasonable quantities of the wood, but at one time there was only enough left to provide work for a further eight weeks. Yet somehow enough walnut was brought in to keep the supply flowing. Altogether a huge amount of money was spent on new buildings and equipment, amounting to just over £270,000, roughly £12 million in today's money. It was worth it. From producing 1,000 rifles per week in 1914, RSAF was turning out over 10,000 per week by 1917, as well as doing rifle repairs, making bayonets and other arms.

The rifle was the weapon issued to every soldier, but it was the machine gun that was to determine much of the course of the war. This was the weapon that literally decimated the troops of both sides as they made their ultimately pointless forays across no-man's-land. Once again, it was an American who led the way towards modern weaponry. Hiram Maxim originally worked on a series of important developments in electric lighting, and it was this that brought him to Europe to an international electrical exhibition in Paris in 1885. He was always on the lookout for new areas to explore and, in a probably apocryphal story, a fellow American told him that the best way to make money from Europeans was to invent something that would make it easier for them to kill each other. In any case, he began to think about machine guns and over the next few years he developed his first weapon. Earlier guns, such as the Gatling, had relied on cranking a handle to bring each round into line. Maxim used a very different method: he realised that the recoil introduced by the exploding gases could be used to eject the used cartridge and bring the next into line. It was purely automatic, but cumbersome. It required a substantial water-cooled jacket to prevent the mechanism from overheating. But it was undeniably effective. Various claims have been made for the firing rate – nominally 600 rounds per minute, though it is doubtful if it ever reached that rate in practice. He set up a factory to manufacture weapons in Britain, financed by a member of the Vickers family. The army were impressed with the results (and found it particularly useful in putting down rebellions in the Empire – Hilaire Belloc, in his satirical long poem *The Modern Traveller*, summed up the situation of the British confronted by what were then popularly regarded as primitive natives: 'Whatever happens, we have got / The Maxim Gun, and they have not').

Vickers were steel manufacturers and were able to make substantial improvements to the gun, but it still remained unwieldy. It was another American, inspired perhaps by his name to turn to invention – Colonel Isaac Newton Lewis – who made the next advance.

He designed a much lighter weapon in 1911, but when the US Army showed no interest he left for Belgium, where he received much more encouragement and the Lewis machine gun went into production. The BSA Company then acquired a licence to manufacture it in Britain. The new machine gun was air cooled instead of water cooled and had a simple two-legged support instead of the Vickers tripod – which could weigh anything up to 50lb. Both guns were to find uses that their inventors had never considered, notably in aircraft: the Lewis was used by observers, who fired it from an open rear position, while the Vickers was the first fixed, forward firing gun (*see* p.169).

The arms manufacturers did not simply rely on weapons and ammunition that existed at the start of the war. They responded to new demands, and one of these came from the increased campaign of Zeppelin raids over Britain. Artillery had not been developed to shoot up into the sky, but the new fighter planes that had come into service during the war could engage with the massive airships. The problem was that the bullets, when they hit, rarely did any real damage. The Zeppelins were kept aloft by a series of gas bags filled with hydrogen. Even if one was punctured the rest could still function. The answer was the incendiary bullet. It was like a conventional bullet, but had a small charge of phosphorus enclosed in the bullet by an airtight plug. On firing, the plug blew out and the phosphorus ignited on contact with the air. The bullet sped on its way, leaving a trail of smoke in its wake. If it was still burning when it hit the Zeppelin, then the result was catastrophic as far as the airship was concerned. Hydrogen is highly inflammable and any fire immediately spread right through the ship. In a famous encounter in August 1918, Major Egbert Cadbury, flying a DH4 biplane, managed to locate the massive L70 Zeppelin. He scored a direct hit and the target was at once engulfed in flames. All the crew were killed, including the captain, Peter Strassen, the man in charge of the whole of the Imperial German Airship Service. There were no more Zeppelin raids on Britain.

The story demonstrates a very important point about the industries of the First World War. A new advance in the technology of the day could have a decisive effect on the whole conduct of the war. It was not just a war between armed services, it was a war between industries and technologies or, as one contemporary put it, a war between Birmingham and Krupp.

The workers in all branches of the arms and munitions industries were stretched to the limit of their abilities and stamina during the war years. But they did have, and needed, some time off, an interlude away from the cares of war, and this narrative will now have its own break from the more serious aspects of the working world.

8

A PEACEFUL INTERLUDE

There was an important industry, employing a large number of people, which didn't make anything tangible, no guns, no ships, no planes, no tanks: but it did provide something essential to the war effort – it cheered people up. This was the entertainment industry. Even in wartime, when the industrial world and its workers were stretched to the limit, there was still a demand for time away from the strains and pressures – and from the bad news of death and injury that came in a relentless and increasing flow from the battlefields. The entertainment industry had its own important part to play in the struggle, and even the government was able to make use of it in its propaganda campaigns to boost morale and encourage extra effort.

In Edwardian England, theatrical entertainment had been divided between what was known as the 'legitimate' stage and the music hall. Everything about them was different. The theatre was respectable, and those in the more expensive seats were expected to turn up in full evening dress. At the start of the war, musical comedies were still popular and three new shows had opened that year; a fourth, *The Cinema Star*, with an excellent cast including the very popular Cicely Courtneidge, closed almost immediately. There was nothing wrong with either the script or the music, but the composer was German.

In 1914 that put it beyond the pale. There were also what were known as 'problem plays', exploring ideas, often inspired by foreign writers such as Ibsen. Among the most successful of the new authors was the socialist George Bernard Shaw whose comedy *Pygmalion* was enjoying a huge success at the outbreak of war. The audiences mostly took it for high comedy and tended to ignore the political message that there is no intrinsic difference between a lady and a flower girl – teach one to speak in the accents of the other and they are indistinguishable. Shaw closed the play on the grounds that theatre was too frivolous for wartime and instead devoted himself to writing pamphlets, such as *Common Sense about the War*. With its underlying argument that Britain was as much responsible for starting the war as the Germans and Austrians, it won him few friends. Theatrical impresarios had different ideas about what the public wanted.

The West End theatres of London were swamped with a patriotic flood of new shows with titles such as *England Expects, On Duty* and *By Jingo, If We Do!* They featured equally patriotic songs – 'Boys in Khaki, Boys in Blue', 'Your King and Country Needs You' and, rather more light-heartedly, 'Sister Susie's Sewing Shirts for Soldiers'. The *Stage Year Book* summed up the mood of the times. What was needed was 'a gaiety that makes one bear with troubles and actual sorrow'. Serious drama was definitely out; the war would 'sweep the boards of finicking problem plays … The nation has had such a stirring-up that the soul-troubles of super-sensitive and over-refined men and women will no longer be of any interest.'[1] Although the patriotic shows were popular, there was also a hunger for pure escapism. By far the most popular show of the war years was the musical *Chu Chin Chow*, roughly based on the story 'Ali Baba and the Forty Thieves'. It opened at His Majesty's Theatre in London on 3 August 1916 and ran for five years. Rather bizarrely for a musical, it was even made into a silent film. Perhaps its loss was not too great: it is now difficult to imagine enthusing over the songs – the show's opening number was 'Here the Oysters Stewed in Honey'.

The provincial theatre was largely dependent on touring companies, and now they faced a whole batch of problems. In the early months of the war, the movement of troops and supplies took precedence over everything else. There was simply no room for actors travelling with their scenery, costumes and props. And to make matters worse, the fare concessions they had enjoyed in the past were removed. Even if they could find space on a train, many companies could no longer afford the fares. There was also a certain pessimism among the impresarios, concerned that the public might not want to leave their homes in such troubled times. But the crisis passed. Trains became available, fare concessions returned and the touring companies were off again. Their main problem now was replacing so many of the young actors who had left to join the forces. There were, however, changes from the pre-war days. It was no longer de rigueur to appear at the theatre in full evening dress. It was less that old barriers were breaking down, but rather more that khaki was as likely to be seen in the stalls as formal black and white.

The music hall was very different: raucous and rowdy rather than sedate and polite. It had reached the height of its popularity at the end of the nineteenth century and was already in decline when war broke out. There were still stars such as Marie Lloyd, Vesta Tilley, Dan Leno and Harry Lauder who could pull in the crowds, but audiences had started to become bored by the all too predictable supporting acts. War brought a revival. People wanted to be cheered up, and the patriotic ticket was just as important in the music hall as in the West End of London. It would be hard to find anyone today who could hum a tune from *Chu Chin Chow*, but the music hall songs of the period are still remembered. Florrie Forde, a music hall singer who could most politely be described as statuesque, had popularised a number of songs, such as 'Down at the Old Bull and Bush' and 'Has Anybody Here Seen Kelly?' But it was another of her songs, written some years before about an Irish boy dreaming of home, that was to be sung and whistled by countless soldiers on their way to the front: 'It's a Long Way to Tipperary'. Many of the other songs of the early war years were far more jingoistic. Some, such as 'Oh We Don't Want to Lose You, but We Think You Ought to Go', were revived in a very different context in *Oh, What a Lovely War!* of 1963, turning the cheerful optimism on its head.

Music hall, however, was never going to keep an enthusiastic audience with popular jingoism alone. People wanted to be entertained, and few impresarios offered more bawdy, slapstick comedy than Fred Karno and his troupe – who were to provide the training ground for two of the great screen comedians, Charlie Chaplin and Stan Laurel. The humour was anarchic – Karno is said to have invented the custard pie in the face – and firmly anti-authoritarian. His company became known as Karno's Army – and the men in the trenches, who by then had learned the reality behind the fine phrases and patriotic songs, added their own words: 'We are Fred Karno's Army, the ragtime infantry, / We cannot fight, we cannot march; what bloody use are we.' Karno, and others like him, added a little gaiety to otherwise grim times.

Popular music was also going through a period of change, with the arrival from America of ragtime, with its new and exciting syncopated rhythm. It was the start of the Jazz Age, though it would be some time before any authentic jazz would reach Britain. The Original Dixieland Jazz Band didn't play in Britain until 1919. What Britain got was the popularised white version of black music, typified by the Irving Berlin song 'Alexander's Ragtime Band'. It was music that spread from the theatre to the dance halls, where new dances such as the 'turkey trot' and the 'bunny hug' offered a less inhibited alternative to the more stately formal ballroom dances. The popular show *Hullo Ragtime!* even had a song 'Farewell to Thee, Dreamy Waltz!' And people no longer had to leave the house to hear the latest tunes: they could listen at home thanks to a brand new invention, the gramophone.

Ragtime was not the only type of music to inspire new dance craze. An older generation frowned on these innovations but reserved their most biting criticism for another import: the slinky, sexy tango. It became immensely popular, but was banned from many dance halls by local authorities as being far too sensuous. It was variously described as 'indecent' and as 'not a dance but an assault'. It did have its supporters, however. One dancer who promoted it was Phyllis Dare, who had herself danced it in the musical *Gaiety Girl*:

Whether it will appear yet awhile at the State Ball and at hunt and country balls, which are proverbially conservative, I should not like to say … Please don't imagine that there is the slightest impropriety about any single movement of the tango as it is danced today. It has long since been rescued from the cabarets of the Argentine and of Montmartre.[2]

The new, popular dances were in fact exactly what the young people needed, whether they were service men home on leave or factory workers having a well-earned rest. The dances were lively, fun and frankly seemed rather sexy – and being banned by puritanical elders made them seem even sexier. Whether in a purpose-built dance hall or in a village hall taken over for a night, a dance offered an opportunity to literally step away for a time from the cares and horrors of warfare.

One other form of entertainment that was to become hugely popular during the war years was a newcomer in the entertainment industry – the cinema. A lot had happened since the Lumière brothers had astonished an audience of just thirty-three Parisians who had paid 1 franc each to see a new attraction at the Grand Café on the Boulevard des Capucines. What they saw was a few shorts, including the now famous *Arrival of a Train at La Ciotat*. Word soon spread, and within a week, 200 eager customers were crowding in to the café – a new entertainment industry had been born. At first, films were shown in fairground booths, but soon spread into a host of little cinemas with titles such as the Bijou and the Gem, which were often no more than converted shops. There was concern about the risk of fire from handling the highly inflammable film stock, so change was enforced by legislation, when the Cinematographic Act of 1909 introduced compulsory licensing of cinemas, which had to comply with strict safety regulations. It also, incidentally, gave local authorities the right to censor or ban films if they were considered indecent. This task was soon to pass to the British Board of Film Censors.

By the time war broke out, the days of the fleapit were ending and the elaborate, highly decorated picture palaces had arrived. It has been estimated that there were between 3,000 and 4,000 cinemas in the country, showing a huge variety of films. Audiences had long since stopped being enthralled by the novelty of simply seeing a moving image. A new industry had grown up, making films that told stories. It was the age of the great silent comedians and the very first film stars. There was a home-grown industry but it was comparatively amateurish. That might all have changed in 1914 when there was a possibility that America might have a powerful impact on the British film industry.

Adolph Zukor had started his working life as a furrier in Chicago, but as a result of a bad debt he acquired a penny arcade and peep-show business. He soon saw the possibilities of the new film medium and began converting his arcades to showing 'motion picture shows'. By 1906 he had left the fur business behind and had helped form one of the most successful of the early film companies – Famous Players – Lasky Corporation. In May 1914 he set up a London studio and sent one of his best directors, Edwin S. Porter – who had made the very first western, *The Great Train Robbery* (1903) – together with a suitably stellar actor, Florence Turner, to start making films. Once the war started, however, the Americans withdrew again, and an opportunity to build an industry was lost. In Britain, the war put an end to such frivolous activities as making entertainment films, and the way was clear for America to dominate the screens of the world. The audiences loved the comedies such as those starring the Keystone Cops, thrilled at serials such as *The Perils of Pauline* and worshipped that new phenomenon, the film star.

There was also, at first, a demand for stories about the war and there was something of a rush of patriotic films with titles such as *The German Spy Peril, Guarding Britain's Secrets* and – one that would be all too true for many families – *Christmas Without Daddy*. As well as fiction, there were actuality films, almost all based on material shot in the UK: *Lord Kitchener's New Army, Ready, Aye Ready* and many more, all sending out a suitably optimistic message. What was largely lacking was any footage revealing what was really going on. Authority was deeply suspicious of the whole idea of actually showing anything directly relating to the war. There is an anecdote, suitably embellished no doubt, about the very rough-diamond American photographer

Merle La Voy who tried to take pictures of war zones and what were considered very sensitive sites, such as Downing Street.[3] He was soon picked up by the police and brought before the head of the CID, Sir Basil Thomson, who had a dossier showing La Voy regularly travelling between London and Paris. Sir Basil demanded to know what was going on, and was told, 'I am photographing the war – that's my game'. Sir Basil was sceptical, until La Voy produced accreditation documents signed by the Vice President of the USA, the Secretary of the United States Navy and the Secretary of War:

> While Sir Basil regarded the letters La Voy started absent-mindedly humming 'The Star Spangled Banner'.
> The dignified Sir Basil was convinced at last.
> 'You may go now.'
> 'Not yet', replied La Voy. 'Now it's my turn. You've been a lot of trouble to me, and I have come all the way over to make some pictures to help England on the screen. It's time you were helping me.

La Voy was soon getting his pictures, but there was no great hurry to encourage anyone else to make pictures to help England on the screen. In spite of official lack of enthusiasm, there was an appetite for another new phenomenon, the newsreel.

Charles Pathé had started in the film business with his brother in the 1890s and by 1902 he had acquired the Lumière studios in Paris and had also set up in London. They started producing the Pathé Gazette, which today seems like a very British institution, but its origins were always to be seen in the crowing French cockerel that opened each episode. Over the war years they were to bring their newsreels to a huge audience, showing not only the war in France, but making a whole series of films on all sorts of war activities on the home front. These are now invaluable resources offering a vivid portrait of wartime Britain.

The government was aware of the value of propaganda, and a special department was set up at Wellington House, London. But when they decided to start making films about the war itself, the proposal was vetoed by the War Office. By 1915 it was clear that the War Office could not keep away forever a world eager for news. The first government propaganda film *Britain Prepared* appeared that December. It was followed by *The Battle of the Somme* that demonstrated the huge appetite of the public for this sort of factual film: within six weeks of its release it had been seen by 20 million people. The films were not aimed just at the local audience: they were also aimed at the neutrals, especially America, who the British hoped to lure into joining them as allies. There, its too blatant message was not so well received.

War documentaries were a very new phenomenon. For hundreds of years, Britain's wars had been fought in someone else's country by professional soldiers, and the public got their information from newspaper reports. Now they could see the action for themselves and witness a war being fought by men who had until recently been friends, neighbours and workmates. Munitions workers could now see exactly what the shells they were making every day were doing; families had a view – albeit a heavily censored one – of what their sons and husbands were enduring at the front. They also saw films of their own working lives, which portrayed them in a splendidly heroic role, cheerfully doing their bit for the mutual effort to win the war.

No doubt these films did a great deal to encourage people, but for the vast majority the cinema offered something very different – an escape from reality into a fantasy world where heroes always triumphed, villains got their just desserts and lovers always ended up in each other's arms. And in a grim world they could laugh, and no one did more to cheer up audiences than Charlie Chaplin. He had begun his film career with Mack Sennett's Keystone Cops, where at first he was just another comic in the crowd. Then, in an otherwise unmemorable movie *Kid Auto Races at Venice*, he chose his own costume and invented a new persona – the little tramp. It was an instant success and propelled Chaplin to the very top of the Hollywood ladder. A new Chaplin film was a tonic that never failed to cheer.

Other popular forms of entertainment fared far less in wartime. Sports, notably football and cricket, attracted huge crowds. The Football Association decided that they would, after all, allow the

FA Cup Final to go ahead in the first year of the war, but moved the venue out of London. The decision to continue playing was not well received. The *Manchester Guardian* editorial made the point that if racecourses were to remain open, why not football grounds, but ended their editorial on a quite different note:

> We fancy none of the other nations engaged in the war feels equally free to amuse itself. And the spectacle of a great part of the able-bodied manhood of England diverting itself with looking on at races and football while our men in France are taking part in a life-or-death struggle is one that brings searchings of conscience.[4]

That was one of the more gentle criticisms. Apoplectic bishops and various disgusted citizens of Tunbridge Wells filled the correspondence columns with complaints. The Cup Final was to be the last match played until after the war. Cricket too came to an end. Test matches were impossible for obvious reasons and county cricket came to an abrupt end, before the season would normally have finished. Surrey won the championship that year, but had to play their final matches at Lord's, as their own ground, the Oval, had been taken over by the military.

Horseracing was badly hit, mainly because there was no transport available to move the horses from stables to racecourses and back again. It seemed likely that as with other sports it would have to stop altogether until the war was over. But racing had always been known as the 'Sport of Kings' – and it seems the title was well earned. George V made it clear that he wanted to continue going to the races – and if the king wanted racing then racing would continue. Yet it was not altogether without interruption. When Aintree racecourse was taken over by the military, the Grand National event had to be cancelled. A similar race was run at Gatwick from 1916 to the end of the war, but was known as the Racecourse Association Steeple Chase, which doesn't have quite the same ring to it.

There was one place of relaxation and entertainment that had been central to the life of the working community for centuries: the pub.

There were always two sides to pub life. There was the pub as a social centre, where people could meet and relax, where there might be games, from skittles and cards to darts and dominoes, and where local affairs could be discussed over a pint of beer or cider. This was the pub celebrated by G.K. Chesterton's 'A Ballade of an Anti-Puritan' in 1915:

> I know where men can still be found.
> Anger and clamorous accord,
> And virtues growing from the ground,
> And fellowship of bed and board,
> And song, that is a sturdy cord,
> And hope, that is a hardy shrub,
> And goodness, that is God's last word –
> Will someone take me to a pub.

There was also the tawdry town pub, with its strict social compartments, from private bar to public bar, as described by Thomas Burke:

> The shabby-flash front, the grime and dull glitter of the interior, the dock-like compartments which screened the customer in one bar from customers in other bars, and even screened him, by an erection of moveable glass shutters, from the staff, and almost made him, when asked for his order, plead Guilty.[5]

Beer drinking in pubs was an integral part of the working life of many industrial regions. Men who had worked in the intense heat of furnaces, in forges and foundries, needed to replace the liquid they had sweated off – and for many years beer was a lot safer than the water. As many were working shifts, pubs near factories would often be open early in the morning for the night shift – and late into the night for everyone else. In many coal-mining districts, payments were made to the butty, a man who represented a small team of workers at the coalface. He would share it out, and often the division would take place in the pub. D.H. Lawrence, who came from a Nottinghamshire mining family, painted a grim picture of home life in his semi-autobiographical novel *Sons and*

Lovers, published in 1913. He described the father coming home drunk, his wages spent and the battles that raged between husband and wife. There was a dichotomy about the pub; a cohesive social place and a destructive source of drunkenness and poverty.

In the pre-war years a strong temperance movement had developed in response to increasing levels of drunkenness, with criminal convictions running at around 200,000 per year. The king publicly announced that he was giving up alcohol for the duration of the war – a lead that was not notably taken up by other members of the upper classes or indeed many others of any class. But the temperance movement did have one very influential supporter in Lloyd George. He had already been one of the key figures behind a government act of 1908 that sought to limit the number of pubs that could be licensed in any one area. In August 1914 he backed the Intoxicating Liquor (Temporary Restriction) Act. This allowed local authorities to limit opening times to a maximum of six hours per day, with a break in the afternoon. It was now up to those authorities to implement the act, which not everyone did, and which called down the wrath of those opposed to the demon drink. To them it was the ultimate evil:

> We all know something of the destruction of life and property caused by the war, we have all read something of the houses and farms and crops shelled and burned; we all know something of the awful loss of life, not only of soldiers but of women and children. Yet tremendous and terrible as is that carnage, it is but a trifle compared with the havoc wrought by drink.[6]

Many pubs now closed their doors as early as 9 p.m., which often gave those who had been working late just an hour or less to have a drink. The result was not always what the government act intended – they crammed an evening's drinking into that one short period, and ended up drunker than they would normally have been.

There was a puritanical and misogynistic strain to the official attitude. In November 1914, the police were told to report any women whose husbands were away fighting and who were seen entering the pub.

They would then have their special allowances stopped. There was particular concern about drink near munitions factories, but official reports on pubs near the Woolwich Arsenal described 'a complete absence of brawling and excitement' and that men and women were 'very good tempered'. In Carlisle, where many of the munitions workers went to the pub on their day off, state-controlled pubs were introduced. There were strict rules about, for example, drinking by persons under the age of 18. They were only allowed drink to accompany food: this apparently resulted in a roaring trade in plates of biscuits. The pubs also offered soft drinks and provided women-only bars.

The government raised duty on beer and reduced its alcoholic content, but that was not considered sufficient to reduce the perceived menace. It was decided that excess drinking was often caused by people buying drinks for each other – or 'treating' as it was officially known. This too was banned by law. The pub survived as a social institution, and beer was still drunk, even if a rather more watery version of the familiar brew. It became known as 'Lloyd George's beer' and even found its way into a music hall song. One verse gives the flavour of it:

> Buy a lot of it, all they've got of it,
> Dip your bread in it, Shove your head in it
> From January to October,
> And I'll bet a penny that you'll still be sober.
> Get your cloth in it, make some broth in it,
> With a pair of mutton chops.
> Drown your dog in it, pop your clogs in it,
> And you'll see some lovely sights in that lovely stuff.[7]

Somehow, in spite of government restrictions, people managed to get some pleasure out of life in the few times they had off from working for the war effort. It refreshed them, and gave them the energy to carry on, no matter how difficult things might become or how gloomy the news from the front.

9

INTERNAL COMBUSTION

The nineteenth century was the great age of the steam engine or, as it could be called, the external combustion engine: the boiler and the fire are separated from the actual moving parts of the engine – they are only there to create the steam that will make the engine work. The alternative idea of internal combustion had been around for a long time. The Dutch scientist Christiaan Huygens had first come up with a somewhat impractical version in the seventeenth century, in which he exploded gunpowder in a cylinder fitted with a piston. The piston was raised and eventually when the gases from the explosion cooled, air pressure forced the piston back down. Apart from the inherent dangers, there was no satisfactory way of constantly adding quantities of gunpowder to the system. What was needed was an explosive substance that could be added with ease whenever necessary. The first answer was to use coal gas, which had become readily available by the middle of the nineteenth century. There were numerous attempts to make a workable engine, but the first big success fell to Nikolaus Otto. He used gas in what became known as the Otto four-stroke cycle – injection, compression, ignition, exhaust – in an engine he built in 1878. He set up the German firm of Otto & Langen, which had considerable success manufacturing all kinds of gas engines. There was one area, however, where there seemed to be no possibility of development and that was transport: the engines had to be attached to a source of gas, which in practice meant the gas main.

The next stage of development was obvious: find a different fuel that could easily be moved around with the engine. The answer was to use some form of oil, and after several experiments by many different engineers, a really successful oil engine based on the Otto cycle was developed by another German engineer, Rudolf Diesel. It was so successful that the name has not only stayed with the engine but with the fuel as well. He took out an English patent in 1892 and now set about convincing the British to use his invention. But he had something of a problem. Britain had huge reserves of coal that could be used in steam engines, but no oil. He attempted to convince the sceptics that in future it would be possible to produce a suitable oil by distilling coal tar:

> Since tar oil can be employed three to five times more efficiently in the Diesel motor than coal in the steam engine, it follows that coal can be much more economically utilized when it is not burned barbarously using boilers or grates, but converted into coke and tar by distillation.[1]

It was not a very convincing argument. In reality it would be oil from the ground that would fuel the new machines, not oil from distillation. It was to prove a major factor in military thinking: why go to a new type of machine, when the fuel supply might be cut off during a war?

The Diesel engine four-stroke operation begins with a downward stroke of the piston, sucking air into the cylinder. At the next upward stroke, the air is compressed and that raises its temperature to over 1,000°F. During the third stroke a mixture of oil and air is forced into the cylinder, and as the temperature in the cylinder is so high the oil ignites. In the final stroke, the burnt gases are expelled from the cylinder. In order to make the engine work, however, it requires that first compression stroke to build up sufficient pressure to cause ignition. On smaller engines this is done manually by winding a starting handle, and as anyone who has tried it can testify, it can be very hard work – and it is easy for the handle to leap back, causing at best a painful strained wrist. The alternative was the hot bulb engine, in which the oil is first heated in a separate bulb using a blowlamp. This seemingly alarming practice would have put off many potential customers for the new engine, but the Diesel salesmen had a special demonstration to reassure them. They poured oil on the floor and threw in a lighted match: the match fizzled out. Once going, however, the cycle is self-perpetuating.

The Diesel engine soon found a use in shipping in many countries, but Britain was very slow to adopt it. Steam was still the preferred source of power in both the Royal Navy and the merchant fleet. But the next advance, again from Germany, began a process that was to sweep the Western world. Working at much the same time, two other German engineers were designing engines that would run on the lighter petroleum fuel. Gottlieb Daimler's petrol engine included a new device, the carburettor, which allowed vaporised fuel to be blown into the cylinder. The other inventor was Karl Benz, who introduced an efficient electrical ignition system. Between them they ensured that a new age in transport was about to begin: the age of the motor car. In 1897 the English Daimler Company began operations in Coventry. The splendidly named *Automotor and Horseless Vehicle Journal* described the new factory:

> The Company's works … comprise a very well lighted factory with offices and stores. The works have railway sidings running trains into them and are moreover close to a canal, and hence raw materials and finished products can be handled with least cost. The factory is well arranged and as far as possible all operations are consecutive, that is the raw material goes in at one end and comes out at the other manufactured into motor cars.[2]

This suggests to a modern reader that the company had a well-organised production line. This was very far from being the case. Daimler, like virtually all the motor manufacturers set up in Britain in the years leading up to the war, worked on a very different system. The all-important engine shop was hardly 'well lighted': what daylight could not provide was still supplied by gas lamps. Each engine was separately built up on a stout iron post set into the floor. The engines would later be taken to the assembly shop. Here, each chassis was laid out on a trestle and the various parts were brought in, and a team of men would gradually build up to the finished car. The various components were mainly made on site using a variety of different processes. Many engine parts would be cast in the foundry, others would be machined. Axles were forged. The bodywork used the technology of the coach builder, with metal panels attached to a wooden frame. The name 'horseless carriage' was altogether appropriate: these early motor cars were simply that, carriages built on traditional lines with a petrol engine replacing the horse. Other more radical ideas soon appeared.

Frederick William Lanchester studied at what was then the Normal School of Science, later to be incorporated into Southampton University. He was already showing an inventive mind and, while still there, took out the first of his 426 patents. He was unimpressed by the academic course, however, and left before completion to take up a job as assistant works manager at the Forward Gas Engine Company in Birmingham in 1888. He must have impressed his employers, for he was still only 20 years old and had no formal qualifications. He soon showed that their judgement had been sound and began making improvements to engine design, starting with a new type of governor. He continued with his inventions for the company, but spent his spare time working on his own ideas. His first interest was in building a heavier-than-air flying machine, but that was a touch too ambitious. He realised that there was no way that a gas engine manufacturer was about to take to the skies, so he turned instead to thinking about motor cars.

In 1891 he developed a single-cylinder 2hp engine that he tried out on a river launch, driving a paddlewheel – a small-scale experiment but it was Britain's first motorboat. After that initial success he began to develop a motor car, based on scientific principles rather than simply adapting old carriage designs. His first attempt, in 1895, contained a number of novel features, and was the first to be built with pneumatic tyres. After a few modifications, he felt that he was ready to go into production and in 1899, after receiving the gold medal from the Automobile Club of Great Britain and Ireland for his design, he and his three brothers set up the Lanchester Engine Company. The production model had many of the new features tried out on the prototypes, including a tubular steel frame and an epicyclic gear, the sort of gear that would appear again much later in automatic cars. It achieved what was, for its time, the very respectable speed of 28mph. Many of the design elements he introduced were to appear in cars produced over the next half-century, but one original feature was fortunately dropped: the first model was steered by a tiller. The changes made by Lanchester were only made possible by comparatively recent advances in technology. The tubular frame is a good example.

In 1885 two German brothers, Max and Reinhard Mannesmann, had invented a new method of making steel tubes. Previously, tubes could only be made by bending a sheet of metal round in a circle and then welding the join, but the tubes invented by the Mannesmann brothers were seamless. A hot steel billet was placed between two rotating rollers set at an angle so that they caused compression in one direction and tension in the other, and that caused the middle of the billet to break open, leaving a central cavity. The rollers drove the billet onto a stationary piercing bar that formed the tube. Apart from their use in car manufacturing, metal tubes were to prove vital components in early aircraft construction.

It was typical of the early years of automobile development that the impetus came not from existing large businesses but from far-sighted individuals. There was, after all, already a thriving construction industry making all kinds of mechanical moving road vehicles. The difference was that they were mostly powered by steam engines, and steam was still considered the best way to move anything, whether on the water, on rails or on the road. Richard Trevithick had invented a steam road carriage as early as 1802 and, by the middle of the nineteenth century, traction engines were being used for road haulage. The early engines all had one thing in common: they required coal to be shovelled into a boiler. Léon Serpollet devised a steam-powered tricycle in 1887 and had gone on to develop steam carriages in which the steam was provided by petrol or paraffin burners, rather than by shovelling coal. The steam car was seen by many as a better bet for the future than the new-fangled internal combustion. Modernity on the road was represented by the electric tramcar that had started to appear on city streets, or the electric train running beneath them in tubes. So it did require a real vision to see that the new machines represented the true way forward.

Two famous companies developed from the same unlikely starting point. The Wolseley Sheep Shearing Machine Company was begun in Sydney, Australia in 1887 and then established a base in Britain. The founder, Frederick York Wolseley, had invented a new sheep-shearing machine and was looking for an engineer to take charge of the works where it would be manufactured. The man he chose was a young Englishman, who had completed his apprenticeship and had come to Australia to work for his uncle's small engineering firm. His name was Herbert Austin. When the company moved to England, Austin went with them, and the business expanded to include the manufacture of machine tools. In 1895 he became interested in the idea of designing motor vehicles and that year he built his first three-wheeler model in his spare time. It had several special features, including a horizontal twin-cylinder engine and, like the Lanchester, a tubular steel frame.

Austin was not satisfied with his first model, and in 1896 built a second three-wheeler in a quite different style. After a few modifications, the new model was fitted with a single-cylinder water-cooled horizontal engine, and had a novel type of improved rear-wheel suspension. It was a slightly odd-looking machine, a two-seater, with the passenger facing the back of the vehicle and the driver facing the front, steering by means of a tiller. Wolseley agreed to start manufacturing the three-wheeler, which made its first public appearance at the cycle show at Crystal Palace in 1896. The company invested

£2,000 in plant and equipment and Austin was able to continue developing new models. His four-wheel 'voiturette' of 1896 won the *Daily Mail* 1,000-mile trial in 1896. The company, however, showed little interest in backing this side of the business, seeing no future in it. They were happy to sell out their new car business, still bearing the name Wolseley, to the mighty armaments manufacturers Vickers and Maxim.

Austin was put in charge of the new Wolseley Tool & Motor Company in 1901, this time with a major capital injection of £40,000. The partnership did not last long. By 1905, Austin had had a major disagreement about engine design with the two Vickers brothers in charge of the parent company. He still favoured the horizontal version instead of the conventional vertical cylinder engine. He managed to get fresh backing from the steel magnate Frank Kayser and set up in business in a former print factory at Longbridge near Birmingham. From a modest start in 1906, when just twenty-three cars were produced, the Austin Company grew rapidly until at the start of the war it was employing over 2,000 staff and producing 1,500 vehicles per year, with engines ranging from 15hp to 60hp and four different body styles, as well as commercial vehicles. Wolseley had also continued to grow after Austin's departure to become by far the most important car manufacturer by the start of the war. So the invention of a sheep-shearing machine in Australia ultimately led to the establishment of two highly successful car makers, Austin and Wolseley.

The early years of the twentieth century had seen a huge burst of activity and innovation. William Morris had been making bicycles and then started repairing motor cars in a modest garage in Oxford, when he decided to start manufacturing and so acquired a factory in Cowley, Oxford. He made his name with the 'bullnose' Morris of 1913. Morris, Austin and Wolseley were all to continue in business for many years more, but other once-mighty manufacturers with great ambition were less fortunate. Argyll cars went into production in Scotland in 1899, and by 1904 they had opened a vast factory at Alexandria, Glasgow, capable of turning out sixty cars per week. Their catalogue for 1907 struck a rather defiant pose:

> Some critics have asserted that the promoters of Argyll Motors Ltd.
> spent too much on appearances, but the few extra hundred pounds
> required to provide a motor car factory second to none in the world
> have been repaid already, by the very advertisement that such a build-
> ing is in itself.

Sadly, it was the critics who were to prove right: by 1913 production at Alexandria was abandoned. Although the company staggered
on for a little while, back on its original, smaller site, it soon closed
down altogether.

What all the early companies had in common was a method of
working, with teams of men each responsible for building an individual car. The great change that was to revolutionise car manufacture
was introduced in America when Henry Ford began making the
famous Model T. This was based on the moving production line, the
conveyor belt. Instead of components being taken to individual cars
spread out around the factory floor, as was being done at the Austin
plant at Longbridge, the car started at one end as a bare chassis, and as
it moved down the conveyor the various parts were added so that it
emerged as a finished car at the end of the process. Now each worker,
spread down the line, was only responsible for his particular compo-
nent: one man might, for example, spend all his working days adding
wheels to axles. Between 1908 and 1927 more than 15 million Model
T Fords were sold worldwide.

The British Ford Company was set up at Trafford Park in 1911 on a
site next to the Manchester Ship Canal that made it easy to bring in
parts from America. In the early days, the cars were built in Detroit,
tested, taken to pieces again and the parts sent on to Britain. By 1914,
a production line had been set up that could turn out twenty-one
vehicles per hour. Compare that with the sixty cars per week from
the Argyll factory and the change could not have been more dramatic. The increased efficiency and concentration on one successful
model made the Model T far cheaper than the alternatives. Ford had
declared that it was his ambition that anyone who had a reasonable
salary would eventually be able to afford a car.

Motor cars were only a part of the production story: there was a growing demand for commercial vehicles of all types. Perhaps the best-known name among the early manufacturers was that of Leyland, which, unusually for the time, was not referring to the name of the man who started the business, but the place of manufacture. The story begins with James Summer, a blacksmith's son with a passion for steam. He built a steam-powered lawnmower that won first prize in a competition organised by the Lancashire Agricultural Society. Encouraged by his success he went into business and became more ambitious, adding his lawnmower engine to a three-wheeled car. He was now joined by two men with experience of steam engines on the railway, George and Henry Spurrier, and together they formed the Lancashire Steam Motor Company at Leyland in 1896. They decided to specialise in making buses, and sold their first steam bus to Dundee City Council. Business grew and by 1905 they had abandoned steam and built their first petrol engine double-decker bus, with the name Leyland stamped on the chassis. They were no longer interested in steam, so they adopted the new name of Leyland Motors Ltd. At first they used engines bought in from Crossley, but were soon manufacturing their own and acquired an important customer: the London & Suburban Omnibus Company.

They were not the only motor-bus manufacturers. The London General Omnibus Company had been formed in 1859 to run a fleet of horse-drawn buses. To face the growing competition from electric trams and the developing underground railway system, the company decided they needed to change to motors, and began by ordering in buses from two manufacturers while they set about the business of designing their own vehicles. Frank Searle had joined the company in 1907 from the Great Western Railway works at Swindon, having decided that the future lay with petrol engines. His first design was the X-type, but he was dissatisfied with some of the details, and made numerous improvements to produce the B-type bus that made its first appearance on London streets in 1910. It had a wooden frame, steel wheels and a chain gearbox. This is the bus that will be familiar to anyone who has ever seen old photos or newsreel of London at the period. It was a double-decker, with a curved external staircase leading to the open upper deck. It carried sixteen passengers inside and eighteen on top at a stately maximum speed of 16mph. By 1913 the company had produced 2,500 B-types. Many working in the War Office would have seen the bus trundling past them and the less exalted would even have travelled on one. Just as it was obvious to the Omnibus Company that the days of horse-drawn passenger vehicles was over, so Whitehall also recognised that this was a more efficient alternative for troop transport. When war broke out, one-third of the entire London General fleet was taken over, with volunteer drivers going with them to France for troop movement. The buses had to be adapted for war use: glass windows were removed and the spaces boarded up, but even so it must have been a shock to some soldiers to find they were travelling to the front on the No. 27 to Paddington. Back in London, more and more women had to be employed to keep the bus services running, working as conductors, clerks and cleaners. By the end of the war there were over 4,000 of them at work.

It was not only people who were being moved around by motor vehicles; several companies were involved in making trucks and vans. The War Office had been happy simply to requisition buses, but in 1912 they recognised that they were also going to need trucks to move supplies of all kinds. They were not convinced that any of the existing models were up to the job, so they decided to try and persuade manufacturers to provide vehicles to their particular specifications. As an incentive they offered a premium on the agreed price and a subsidy for three years at £20 per annum. In the event of war the vehicles had to be made available at seventy-two hours' notice and the army agreed to purchase them at market value plus 25 per cent. It did not receive a very positive response from most manufacturers, as one anonymous company director explained:

> There were a number of reasons for this, but the chief reason probably lay in the fact that the special subsidy type of motor lorry was expensive in design, and that it did not lend itself readily to trade purposes for which other types of chassis and bodies had been found more suitable. The inducement offered by the authorities was also insufficient.[3]

In other words, it was all very well designing what the army wanted, but if there was no war they would be stuck making vehicles that didn't fit peacetime needs. Leyland was one of the few who applied and they won contracts in the 30cwt and 3-ton class; by 1913 they had increased their workforce to 1,500. By the start of the war they had made 2,000 vehicles and during the war years they produced 6,000 vehicles. They were not the only manufacturers who recognised that there would be a profitable business in supplying the military. John Thorneycroft Ltd of Basingstoke had, like Leyland, started in business producing steam-powered vehicles, but had switched to motors in 1902. They produced their J-type lorry specifically to meet War Office criteria. The 4-ton lorry was to become the workhorse of the army, with over 5,000 going into production. But although they had been approved by the War Office, they had to overcome a certain reluctance among the generals, who at first preferred wagons pulled by tractors: they were more like the horse-drawn carts they were used to. The Albion Motor Company of Scotland was another major supplier, building 6,000 lorries for the services with 32hp engines.

The commercial vehicle manufacturers thrived during the war years as there was a steady and increasing demand for their vehicles. It had not been obvious at the start that this would be the case: no one was sure whether the army actually wanted to use vehicles and, if they did, whether there would be a profit for their manufacturers. A hint of army attitudes could be found at the huge annual army exercises held in 1913: 45,000 men were deployed, 17,000 horses took to the field, 2,220 horse-drawn vehicles were in use but a mere 192 motor vehicles were present, and many of those were staff cars to ferry the officers around.

However, by the start of the war the need for motor vehicles was too obvious to be ignored. The change was dramatic, but it did not benefit all companies, and there were soon grumblings among manufacturers. In August 1914 government inspectors did the rounds of all motor manufacturers and issued instructions on exactly what they were to produce. At first, contracts were issued with the rather farcical proviso that they were subject to cancellation at just three weeks' notice, though this was later increased to six weeks. Even then it is impossible to imagine setting up a production line for a new venture under such terms. Worse was to follow as far as the manufacturers were concerned, with the introduction of the Munitions Act of 1915, which made the motor manufacturers 'Controlled Establishments'. This was the act under which trade unions agreed not to strike and to accept dilution. In return for union concessions, industries involved would not be allowed to benefit financially in terms of extra profits that would come from keeping wage bills low for male workers and employing large numbers of women, mostly at far lower pay rates. The motor industry argued that it had no arguments with unions and did not employ women, but it was still being expected to pay extra taxes on greater profits, when in reality the alleged profits actually represented capital that was being invested in making the necessary vehicles for war. The anonymous company director quoted below was vehement in his condemnation:

> It is not the least extravagant to say that, if the balance sheets of practically all the companies engaged in the heavy vehicle industry were taken and adjusted upon the bare allowance of the Act, there is not one which would survive to find the necessary money to meet the 'excess' profit tax.

The disaster did not strike as predicted among the commercial vehicle manufacturers, but the car manufacturers were in a very different situation.

At the start of the war in 1914, Britain was ready to embrace a new and powerful motor manufacturing industry – and then everything changed. Motor cars were luxuries: even the cheapest available, the Model T Ford, cost £152: that represented almost eighteen months' wages to a labourer in a munitions factory at the start of the war, and other models were considerably more expensive. Car production was not considered essential and virtually came to a complete standstill. Even those who had vehicles found it all but impossible to get petrol to fill them, so there was no demand for new cars. Some of those who had already bought cars or vans found ingenious solutions to the problem, one of which was to convert the engine to using gas as a fuel. This was usually achieved by filling a large bag with gas from the mains and strapping it to the top of the vehicle. It was never a very satisfactory answer. Owners of commercial vehicles often didn't have such problems: many were requisitioned for the forces and trundled off to France and Belgium.

Government inspectors now told companies just what they were expected to manufacture instead of cars. The situation at the new Austin plant at Longbridge was typical, with most of the works now given over to manufacturing shells and armament, and later aeroplanes. Austin did try to make use of their expertise in manufacturing light vehicles by designing an armoured car, known as the 'Dreadnought'. He was not the first to hit on such an idea. Frederick Simms had designed what he called a 'Motor-war car' using a Daimler engine, with armour-plated body and armed with a Maxim machine gun. He demonstrated it to the War Office who were unimpressed, Lord Kitchener dismissing it as 'a pretty mechanical toy'. The Austin version was based on one of their standard car chassis, with an armoured body, complete with two turrets, each capable of mounting a machine gun. The vehicle could be driven from either end. The British Army was not interested, so the Dreadnoughts were sent abroad, mainly to Russia. Changes had to be made, as the armour – which was only intended to be bullet-proof and shrapnel-proof – turned out to be inadequate and had to be replaced. In its original form it was said to be capable of speeds of 50mph, but the heavier armour slowed it down. The speeds were, in any case, only given for travel on 'good roads'. That was exactly what the Western Front mainly lacked. For a vehicle to be really useful on the battlefield it needed to be specially designed using quite different principles. How that was done is another, very convoluted and intriguing story.

10

WATER CARRIERS FOR MESOPOTAMIA

The answer to the problem of making a machine that could cross almost any terrain, no matter how muddy and waterlogged, and even cross open trenches, had a long period of gestation. It owed its original development, however, not to the demands of the battlefield but to the more peaceful world of farming. Traction engines had been in use throughout the nineteenth century, but they had limitations in agriculture simply because of the weight of the wheeled machines creating deep ruts in the soil. Rubber production did not really begin in Britain until the middle of the nineteenth century, and it was to be even later before the inflated tyre came into use. So, if a heavy machine was not going to ruin the land it ran across, then an alternative idea was needed. The eventual answer would be what we now call a caterpillar track. In fact, the basis for the eventual design had been proposed as early as 1770 by Richard Edgeworth, even before the invention of the traction engine. He took out a patent for a 'portable railway and artificial road to move along with any carriage to which it is attached', but it never became a working machine. In 1825 Sir George Cayley, who is best known as one of the very first pioneers of flight by heavier-than-air planes, produced a much improved version of the Edgeworth original. He placed a flexible band of joined metal plates that passed round the wheels of a traction engine to provide drive, with smaller wheels in between to help carry the load. This was a genuine caterpillar track. Various other versions appeared over the years. John Boydell produced a less elegant version, which consisted of four or five metal plates fastened to the outside of the drive wheels that flopped down as the wheels turned. Surprisingly, the Boydell system was considered the better of the two by the engineers of the day, and it was to be the Boydell steam tractor that was put to work in the Crimean War. Like the majority of traction engines of the day, it originally required a horse to walk in front, not to pull the engine but to steer it. Later versions had a single wheel in front, which could be turned by a steersman perched just behind it. The use of a steering wheel working through chains to the front axle had not yet been developed for traction engines: it made its first appearance on a steam roller. In wartime conditions, the job of steersman must have been almost impossibly dangerous, stuck out in front of the slowly trundling machine with no protection whatsoever. The new machines never came into general use with the army.[1]

The next stage of development of powered army vehicles came about because the military had decided rather belatedly, 100 years after the first steam locomotive had appeared on Britain's roads, that there might be a place for a steam tractor to work alongside their horses to move artillery. It was not a new idea. A Frenchman, Nicholas-Joseph Cugnot, who had been an officer in the Austro-Hungarian Army, had seen the need for such a vehicle when he served in the Seven Years' War in the 1760s. On his retirement, he built a steam tractor specifically designed for hauling artillery. It was tried in the streets of Paris in 1769, but literally ran into a brick wall and the whole idea was forgotten. So it was in the twentieth century, not the eighteenth, that the British Army turned to the idea of a mechanical artillery tractor. They set up the Mechanical Transport Committee (MTC) to investigate the matter. The MTC were, however, aware that there was a problem with the steam engines not being able to travel long distances without stopping to take on water, but felt that the problem could be overcome. In 1902 they offered a prize of £1,000 for a tractor that could haul a 25-ton load for 40 miles without stopping. They do not seem to have considered anything much beyond a conventional steam traction engine: the alternative, the motor tractor, was developed because a commercial manufacturer decided that it would be a good, and potentially profitable, idea.

Richard Hornsby had set up a company making agricultural machinery early in the nineteenth century. He took a very pragmatic view of how best to develop new ideas. He bought a farm near his works, and all prototypes were tested there before going into production. By the early twentieth century, the managing director and chief engineer at Hornsby was David Roberts, who decided to try for the War Office prize. In 1904 he submitted a conventional traction engine, except that it was powered by a 70hp oil engine instead of by steam. It successfully completed the course, and went a further 18 miles, winning the company a small bonus. The army purchased the machine, but did not order more. Roberts was not convinced, however, that this was really capable of doing the job of hauling guns over rough, muddy ground in wartime conditions. In 1904 he took out a patent for what he called a 'chain-track' vehicle, a form of caterpillar tractor powered by a paraffin engine. A lightweight version was also fitted to a Rochet-Schneider motor car.

In 1906 Roberts gave an unofficial demonstration of the new machine to members of the MTC at the company's works at Grantham. It was not a complete success. The engine proved hopelessly underpowered and the steel frame flexed, sending the bearings out of alignment and stalling the engine. The prototype did, however, cross a 4ft-wide trench, a feat that would prove highly significant for future developments, and managed a series of other obstacles that defeated a conventional steam tractor. The MTC recognised the shortcomings but also appreciated its potential. In their report they wrote:

> This tractor demonstrated to the Committee its peculiar power to move over ground that would bring any tractor fitted with ordinary wheels to a standstill … the Committee are of opinion that this vehicle rough

though it is, and unsuitable though its engine may be, is in its power of traversing ground difficult and even impossible to other engines, a marked advance on anything that has heretofore been manufactured.[2]

Encouraged by the trial, the MTC asked Roberts to fit his chain drive to the original tractor they had bought from him in 1904, which at least had enough power to do the job. He added an improved track system and gave a demonstration at the army base at Aldershot. It was there that the soldiers renamed the chain tracks – they called them caterpillars, and the name stuck. Roberts now suggested that the machine could be adapted to haul a caterpillar-tracked gun carriage. They gave a prestigious display at the royal review at Aldershot in 1908 in the presence of the king and the Prince of Wales. It was an outstanding success, and Roberts showed that he had a keen grasp of the value of the modern publicity available at the time by shooting a propaganda film, in which a horse and cart sank into marshy land and were hauled out by the new tractor. It was shown to cinema audiences and taken on the rounds of embassies and military attachés. The MTC were thoroughly satisfied that Roberts and Hornsby had come up with exactly what they had been briefed to find: an efficient tractor suitable for military use. Now all they had to do was convince the officers of the Royal Artillery if not yet to abandon their horse-drawn gun carriages, at least to try the new machine alongside them. That was to prove a far more difficult task.

Hornsby continued to make improvements and a third version was given trials at Aldershot and it was then that one of the MTC, Major Donohue, suggested the idea of doing away with the second gun carriage, and mounting the gun directly onto just the one caterpillar track vehicle. Roberts never took the hint. In the meantime, further trials against conventional horse-drawn gun carriages took place and the artillery officers were unimpressed. They objected to the noise and the smell and, in an echo of Victorian objections to the motor car, complained that it would frighten the horses. The MTC responded to the criticism by pointing out that the whole point of the new vehicle was that it should be there ready to take over where horses couldn't cope – mechanised tractors and horses weren't supposed to meet, so the problem wouldn't arise. The other arguments – underpowered, noisy and smelly – could all be sorted out during the development process.

There was a new attempt to convince the army: a third model was tested in 1911 with a more powerful engine, resulting in a machine that could travel twice as fast as its predecessor. The MTC were still sure that trials against horses would show the huge advantages that mechanisation could bring. There was now a new Director of Artillery, Brigadier General Stanley von Donop. He showed no enthusiasm for mechanisation and seemed more than happy to continue using horses, despite the cogent arguments put up by the MTC. For Roberts, it was the final straw. He had spent five years developing and improving his tractor, at considerable cost to the company, and he was reluctant to invest any further capital in the face of such discouragement. It was not only the military that showed no interest: there was no civilian demand either. He decided to cut his losses and sold his patents to the Holt Company of America for £4,000. Holt took the popular name as a trademark and when they merged with C.L. Best in 1911 the new company was registered as the Caterpillar Tractor Company. An important British initiative had been lost and the army, having seemed to take a step forward into the twentieth century, lurched back into the nineteenth. It was still to be the age of the horse, not the horseless carriage. That was the situation when war broke out.

Colonel Holden, who had been one of the most enthusiastic members of the MTC team, was appointed assistant director in charge of mechanical transport supplies. With Hornsby out of the running, Holden, who had remained an enthusiastic advocate of the caterpillar tractor, was forced to buy in a model from Holt in America for trials. Over the war years nearly 2,000 Holt tractors had to be imported at great cost in both money and in the use of valuable shipping space. With foresight and without the obstinate insistence of the artillery officers to stick with the familiar that need could all have been supplied by British companies. The decision to stay with horses probably looked sensible in terms of the fast-moving campaigns that the generals had planned and expected: it was a good deal less so in the war of attrition that spread along the Western Front. Now a new imperative became uppermost in the military planners' thinking: what can we do to overwhelm the enemy trenches?

Various devices were tried out that would demolish the fortifications of the enemy trenches, including a form of water cannon, but none were effective. At least one voice was raised loudly proclaiming that something needed to be done. Lt Col Ernest Dunlop Swinton was appointed as official war correspondent at the end of 1914. He was in fact the only correspondent allowed to go anywhere near the front line, but what he saw dismayed him. Like other British Army officers he was astonished and horrified by the destructive power of the German machine guns. It was, he said, 'a revelation' – and he began investigating ideas on how the enemy trenches could be attacked without huge troop losses. The answer he came up with was some form of armed caterpillar track vehicle that could roll straight through the barbed wire defences to attack gun positions. He took his idea to Capt. Maurice Hankey, secretary to the Committee for Imperial Defence. Both Swinton and Hankey tried to interest Lord Kitchener in the idea and both later gave evidence at a civil trial on who really had devised this new form of vehicle and what the official reaction had been:

> Sir Dunlop Swinton spoke of the great difficulties in overcoming machine-guns and barbed wire, and he said he thought the Holt tractor might be adapted to overcome them. He agreed to try and interest people at home in the matter and he spoke twice about it to Lord Kitchener, who never referred to any information he might have had on the subject. Lord Kitchener was unreceptive to the idea – and he failed to catch Lord Kitchener's imagination.[3]

At the same hearing, Hankey told a similar tale of trying to forward the idea with War Office officials, with no more success, ending as Swinton had with Kitchener who simply announced that the 'armoured caterpillars would be shot up by guns'. His final comment was: 'I was stymied.'

With the army apparently showing no interest in new ideas, Hankey drafted his ideas in a memorandum that he wrote over the Christmas period of 1914. He began with a plea for new thinking: 'Is it possible by the provision of special material to overcome the present impasse? Can modern science do nothing more?'[4] He went on to propose all kinds of devices, from bullet-proof shields to be pushed forward ahead of the infantry to rocket-propelled grapnel hooks to grasp the barbed wire and drag it down. Top of the list was the favourite device, the armed caterpillar vehicle. This time the note not only went to Kitchener but also to the head of the Admiralty, Winston Churchill. On the face of it, the navy should not have been concerned in the matter at all but, with the army seemingly reluctant to modernise, Churchill began to take the initiative. He had allies.

Colonel R.E.B. Crompton was a veteran engineer who had for a long time been arguing that it was foolish of the army to rely for its transport on small-wheeled lorries that could only be used on decent roads. Like others, he made the case for caterpillar tracks. He was baulked by Col Holden, also of the MTC, who dismissed the idea more or less out of hand. Crompton was scathing, and wrote to Holden in September 1914. He pointed out that as the only mechanical engineer on the MTC it was his duty to ensure that correct decisions were taken about the transport that the army was going to need. The current position depended on the assumption that the army would always have hard roads on which to run their vehicles, yet this was quite clearly not the case. Transport would eventually be floundering in the mud. He ended in the most uncompromising way:

To put it quite plainly to you. I think everyone will hold you responsible as technical adviser to the War Office for the type of wagon that is now in use and you will incur serious responsibility if you ignore what I now tell you is practically certain to take place under existing conditions.

He had no more success than others in persuading the army, but he had more luck among the officers of the Royal Naval Division. One of these was Col Wilfred Dumble, who had left the army in 1907 to manage the innovative London General Omnibus Company and had already shown his initiative by organising the first fleet of London buses to arrive in France. He had seen the transport problem at first hand and shared Crompton's view of the way forward. Just as the early development of caterpillar tracks had come from a manufacturer who had started in the traction engine business, so now the two men went to consult another major manufacturer in that field, William Foster & Co. of Lincoln. The general manager, William Ashbee Tritton, had already produced a successful wide-wheeled tractor for hauling 16in howitzers. He seemed the obvious choice as a possible manufacturer for a new generation of vehicles.

Churchill at once began to show an interest in what had become known as the howitzer tractor, which had demonstrated an ability to cross trenches on its vast wheels. He conceived the idea of adapting it as a trench-bridging machine. It would carry men, and on reaching a trench would lay its own bridge across. Work had hardly gone beyond consideration of the idea when Churchill changed his mind – what was really wanted was an armoured vehicle that could go anywhere and would be the equivalent of a naval battleship: a landship. He set up the Landships Committee in February 1915. The first meeting was attended by Tritton and Dumble, together with Capt. Tommy Hetherington, one of the pioneers of military aviation, a representative of the Coventry ordnance factory and the magnificently named Eustace Tennyson d'Eyncourt. Although the latter had a typical upper-class background, educated at Charterhouse public school, he declined to follow the expected route to Oxford. His gifts were more practical than academic, so instead of university he took a five-year apprenticeship at the Armstrong Whitworth works at Elswick on the Tyne. In order to broaden his experience, he moved from there to the Fairfield yard on the Clyde to learn about the manufacture of merchant shipping. In 1902 he was invited back to Elswick to head their design department and ten years later he was appointed by the

Admiralty to the post of Director of Naval Construction. He was very effective in his new role and was even involved in the early development of rigid airships for the navy. He was to use his vast experience in warship design to good effect in the development of landships. Dumble soon suggested that Crompton should also be consulted as an expert on heavy vehicle construction, and he was added to the team.

Churchill was well aware of the lack of enthusiasm for such projects at the War Office that, in the case of many of the leading figures, amounted to outright hostility. It was an attitude that went right to the top of the War Cabinet where Kitchener himself was notably opposed to change. Persuading them to back this initiative would have been difficult if not impossible, so Churchill decided simply to bypass them altogether. He kept the Landships Committee as his own concern: not even Kitchener was let into the secret.

The committee decided at the beginning to investigate the two obvious alternatives: large-wheeled and tracked vehicles. Tritton was understandably very much in favour of the large-wheeled vehicles that he had already been developing for the bridge-laying machine. As he went ahead thinking about new designs to meet Churchill's objectives, a new machine appeared in London. Crompton was told that William Strait of the Killen Strait Manufacturing Company of Wisconsin was in town and willing to demonstrate their new lightweight tractor. This had two caterpillar tracks at the side for power and a third track at the front for steering. Crompton bought the machine and put it through various tests and trials, though he remained convinced that the wheeled vehicles were superior.

The various tests and designs had to be kept secret, so they were all carried out under the unlikely disguise that what was being developed was a water carrier destined for use in Mesopotamia. The workers at Foster's got tired of constantly using this cumbersome title in all their documents, so shortened it to water tank and eventually the project simply became known as building tanks – and the vehicles finally had a name that would stick.

The whole project was plagued by both technical and political difficulties. No one was agreed on what the landship should be, how it would operate and whether a large-wheeled or tracked vehicle was preferable. Work had barely got under way before it became clear that Churchill's campaign at Gallipoli was a disaster. The result was that Churchill was ousted from the Admiralty and his place taken by Arthur Balfour. The Sea Lords were not only not in favour of continuing the landship programme, but some were vehemently opposed. Commodore Lambert put it bluntly: 'Caterpillar landships are idiotic and useless. Nobody has asked for them and nobody wants them.' Balfour simply referred to them as 'Churchill's fad'. It seemed that the whole project was doomed, but Churchill managed to persuade Balfour to at least keep the Landship Committee going until one vehicle had been built and could be given a fair trial.

Tritton had been wholly in favour of the large-wheeled version, but he was overruled. He was hugely disappointed, but had a consolation prize: Foster was given the task of building the prototype. By now the army had become involved in the project and had set out their conditions. The vehicle should be capable of a speed of not less than 4mph on the flat and not less than 2mph when climbing. It should be able to turn through ninety degrees and be able to cross gaps up to 5ft width and parapets up to 5ft high. It was to be capable of carrying ten men, with two machine guns and one light gun. The first prototype was ready by September 1915. Nicknamed 'Little Willie', it was not an immense success. It was little more than an armoured box sat on top of American caterpillar tracks, powered by a Daimler engine. The tracks proved liable to come off on rough ground and it never achieved the required speed, only reaching a modest 3mph. Work began at once on a new version, known as 'Mother'. This was a very different design, with the caterpillar tracks wrapped right round the sides of the tank.

In January 1916, Mother was sent down to Hatfield – with Little Willie as first reserve – under conditions of great secrecy, for official trials. Kitchener, the great sceptic, was there and he was given a personal demonstration in the morning. Tritton later recalled his reaction, saying that he had talked to Kitchener for about an hour and had come away 'very depressed'.[5] Kitchener left before the full trial was completed in the afternoon. Tritton said he remembered Lord Kitchener's use of the phrase: 'It is a pretty mechanical toy'. Others were more enthusiastic. Churchill, who had so vigorously promoted the programme, was not there, but d'Eyncourt was able to write to him just a few days later: 'It is with great pleasure that I am now able to report to you that the War Office have at last ordered 100 landships to the pattern which underwent most successful trials recently.' The tank had arrived.

Over the next two years, there were to be many design improvements and many different companies were to become involved in tank manufacturing. Foster continued to have a substantial role, supplying the army with over 400 tanks altogether, but the most important constructor turned out to be the Metropolitan Railway Carriage and Wagon Company of Birmingham, which had been formed in 1863 to do exactly what their name suggests. They had just the right sort of equipment for the job, and they shared with Foster the work of supplying the first generation of tanks, the Mk I, based on the original Mother vehicle.

Metropolitan were not the easiest company to deal with. The chairman, Dudley Docker, was highly suspicious of the military, being convinced that if he allowed their engineers to see his books they would end up passing secrets to civilian rivals. His mistrust of the military may have been misplaced in that respect, but in other ways it proved all too well founded. The ministry, while demanding ever more tanks, also removed the exemption from service status of many of the key workers in the factory. This had to be overcome by drafting engineers, who had already been called up, back into the works. Over the next two years even more complications were to make life difficult. The army seemed to have little or no understanding of production processes, and thought that whenever they had a better idea for a new design they had only to pass on their requirements for them to be instantly applied. This proved particularly troubling when it came to building the later Mk IV and Mk V versions. Metropolitan had to point out at one stage that they were tooled up ready for production and if they made the changes the army now wanted, everything would have to come to a complete halt to prepare for work on a new design. Lucien Legros, the president of the Institution of Automobile Engineers, put it firmly in a presidential address to the institution in 1916. This, he said, was an engineer's war, yet the army had no qualified chief mechanical engineer, and the engineers who did work for the army were put under the control of officers less qualified for the job than the men under them. In spite of all the production difficulties, Metropolitan turned out nearly 200 Mk IV tanks and over 1,000 Mk V. The tanks were coming out of the factories – now it was up to the army to use them to good effect.

Tanks first went into battle at Flers in France and, according to *The Times* correspondent, when the German soldiers 'looked towards the English their blood froze in their veins as two mysterious monsters came creeping over the crater fields'. Yet it was not until the end of 1917 that tanks were used en masse in a major offensive at the Battle of Cambrai. In twelve hours the British Army had advanced for 10,000 yards, which may not sound a huge amount until you compare it with what was intended as the major offensive of the war, the Third Battle of Ypres, where it had taken three months and hundreds of thousands of casualties to achieve as great a gain. Even then, many of the older officers were unconvinced and still hankered after the old days of dashing cavalry advances. As late as 1921 Brigadier General Haig was still proclaiming that 'the cavalry will never be scrapped to make room for the tanks'. Fortunately, there were many who disagreed, and production rose steadily; from a modest 150 tanks produced during 1916, over 2,500 were turned out in the last two years of the war.

Like many of the stories of the First World War this one can be seen as one featuring the reactionary old brigade refusing to accept new technology. But it is rather more than that. It is also a story that exemplifies the way in which industrialists did far more than just supply what the armed forces declared they need: they were also innovators in their own right. Had anyone been prepared to listen to Hornsby's ideas in the first place, then the whole course of the war might have been very different. And when development eventually did get under way, the importance of Tritton and Foster's contributions cannot be overestimated. Nor can the importance of the tank in the final offences. Haig, whatever his doubts, wrote at the end of the war that tanks were then being used on every battlefield: 'And the importance of the part played by them in breaking up the resistance of the German infantry can scarcely be exaggerated'. That success was due to a few far-sighted officers in both the army and the navy and the industrialists of Britain.

11

SHIPBUILDING

The British shipbuilding industry at the start of the twentieth century had entered what many would regard as a golden age. There had been huge technical advances, typified by two great liners, specifically designed to take and hold the Blue Riband, the trophy awarded for the fastest ships on the transatlantic crossings. The RMS *Mauretania* was built by Swan Hunter on the Tyne and the RMS *Lusitania* by John Brown on the Clyde. They represented all that was best in modern shipbuilding practice. There were exacting safety standards, which demanded a stress factor of 3.5. A factor of 1 meant that the ship had to be able to withstand the impact of a wave equal in length to the length of the ship and a height of 1:20 of the length. In the case of the *Mauretania* the 3.5 specification meant it would have to withstand a wave of over 2,600ft long and 130ft high. It can safely be said that no sea captain ever expected to meet such a monster. Even before work started at Swan Hunter there were two years of testing the hull design, first with models in a test tank and then using an electric launch in a closed dock. While this was going on, the company set about improving the yard, with a new 750ft-long construction shed, fitted with overhead electric cranes. All the latest technological advances were incorporated: high tensile steel was used and plates were riveted together using a new form of mild steel rivet, heated in an electric furnace and hammered into place with pneumatic riveters. The engines too were of the very latest design: four giant turbines for forward drive and two more for going in reverse. Four turbo-generators provided enough electric power to run a town with a population of 100,000. The ship may not have had that big a population, but when fully booked and staffed, it would be carrying over 2,000 passengers and over 800 crew. The *Mauretania* duly took the Blue Riband in 1907 with an average speed for the crossing of almost 24 knots, a record it was to hold for another twenty-two years.

Great liners such as the *Mauretania* and *Lusitania* were high-prestige vessels, but the true measure of Britain's dominance lay in the huge range of vessels being built. The British merchant fleet was the biggest in the world and its ships were built in British yards. The Royal Navy had the most powerful fleet in the world, and both private and naval dockyards were kept fully at work. The new generation of warships, like the great liners, incorporated new technology. The navy had been slow to move away from the age of the wooden sailing ships firing broadside, but by the start of the twentieth century, the revolution was complete. The First Sea Lord, Lord Fisher, early in his career had commanded what was then the most advanced warship of its day: the *Inflexible*, laid down in 1876. It was fast for its time with a top speed of over 12 knots and carried four 81-ton guns that could be fired ahead and astern at the same time. Over thirty years later, once he was in a position to dictate naval strategy, he ordered the construction of an even more impressive class of battleship, starting with *Dreadnought*. According to the official history of one of the yards building this class of vessel: 'She was far ahead in design of anything previously built, and the secrecy with which the work was carried out gave Britain two years' advantage over German naval designers.'[1] It was a huge ship, 490ft long and 82ft beam, with impressive armament. It carried three pairs of 12in guns mounted on three turrets on the centre line, and two more turrets on the broadside. It was the first battleship to be fitted with steam turbines, which gave it a speed of 21 knots. Where protection was most needed, amidships, it was clad in 11in-thick armour plating.

The production of armour plating of this thickness was no easy matter. What started as a vast ingot or billet of steel had to be squeezed out between iron rollers, much as a lump of dough is flattened in a pasta-making machine. To make such a system work required a great deal of power, such as from the steam engine now preserved in the industrial museum at Kelham Island, Sheffield (described in chapter 6). So it would seem as war broke out that the shipbuilding industry was modern, progressive and ready to take on whatever tasks were needed. In a sense this was true, but advances in technology had not been matched by advances in working practices.

The first problem lay with the way in which work was organised in the yard. Rather as in the early motor industry, there was no steady flow of materials. Steel was sent in sheets from the strip-rolling mill. Each piece was then individually painted with an identification number, after which it joined others in the holding racks waiting until it was needed. From there it was taken to the marking gantry, where the positions for the holes for the rivets were marked out. The actual punching of the holes required a gang of six helpers to manhandle the sheet for the punching plater. It was then swung across to another bed for the holes to be counterpunched. Then the plate was moved by another squad of six men to the 'hanging-up plater'. There the sheet was planed and, if necessary, bent to the appropriate shape for its position on the hull. Only then was it ready to be taken to the erection berth. At this time virtually all ships were built out in the open and the work of fastening the sheets to the frame and to each other was the work of riveters. Basically, the two pieces of metal to be riveted had to be positioned so that the previously drilled holes were in alignment. The rivet itself consisted of a cylindrical section, the same size as the hole, with a larger mushroom-shaped head. Once the rivet had been pushed through the two holes, with the head resting against one of the plates, the other protruding end had to be hammered over and flattened out against the second plate, holding the two firmly together.

Although pneumatic riveting was used in the more progressive yards, some still stuck with the old method of hammering the rivets home by hand. But the real trouble came from the cumbersome system of allocating the necessary work, as was explained in a history of the industry written just a few years after the end of the war.[2] The old-fashioned riveting gang consisted of a gang of five workers. The 'boy' – always a boy no matter how old – heated the rivets in a portable brazier and threw them to the 'catcher'. From him it went to the 'holder up' who put the rivet in place and held it there. Standing on the opposite side of the two sheets of metal from the holder up were the riveters, who struck the rivet with alternate blows to flatten out the end over the plate. This seems extraordinarily complex, especially when you consider that a large battleship would contain literally millions of rivets. Yet it seems that introducing pneumatic riveting did not always increase efficiency: 'Sections of the pneumatic plant cannot be run at a profit, nor, as compared with hand power, is there an appreciable increase in output.' It was an old argument in the shipyards: it is easier to keep costs down by hiring cheap manual labour than by investing in new machinery.

Even with the new system in place, the riveters had to rely on others to prepare the work ready for them to do their bit. The work had to be screwed up, and if the holes had not been correctly positioned in the first place, which often turned out to be the case, a driller had to be called in to make new holes and then another worker called in to countersink them. The system could scarcely be called a model of streamlined efficiency, and to make matters worse, the conditions under which the men worked were atrocious. A former shipyard worker on the Clyde, Daniel Murray, recalled those days:

> And many a time ye watched the riveters riveting all day just in their, just in their trousers, no shirt or nothin' on. The sweat was pourin' out them, knockin' in rivets, thousands a day. And they used tae have a big pail beside them wi' water in it and meal. Meal fur tae make a drink ye know, fur when they were thirsty. A riveter was a hard job, no doubt about it. They were worth a' the money, the riveters.[3]

To Murray, however, this was not the worst job in the yard. That dubious privilege went to screwing up, positioning plates on the hull, ready for riveting. Often this involved standing on a cradle, consisting of nothing more than a couple of planks suspended by ropes, swinging around beneath the curve of the hull. It was from this precarious position that the men had to work with the heavy, unwieldy plates, while others might be working overhead. Safety was not a priority:

> Oh safety, there was no safety precautions in them days. You just worked, you had on whatever you had, just a cap, that's all you had, just a cap on your head. Say in them days if anything struck you on the head your head split open. Many a time we were hurted that way, you know.
>
> Shoes? You never got anythin', nothin'! You'd to buy your own. You never got supplied wi' nothin' in the shipyard. Nothin'. All we wore was a pair o' overalls an' eh, just yer jacket. Maybe a pullover and yer' jacket on the top, that was all ye had. You never got any gloves or nothin' in them days to cover your hands or that. A' we had ta dae was we made a pair o' leathers wursel' fur yer hands, ye know. You got a bit of o' leather out and you cut, you slit a hole in it and you put yer hand though it an' that gave ye a grip. If you hadn't them when ye were shearin' the plates yer hands used tae be all cuts. A plate's like a razor. See when a plates cut wi' the shears, they were very sharp. They were very sharp. They cut yer hands. Many a time yer hand was a' jaggy and cuts wi' it.

The workers on the berth were exposed to the weather and that created its own problems. George Bartram of Bartram & Sons of Sunderland kept a wartime diary.[4] In February 1916, for example, work was stopped and the men demanded a quarter's day pay for the hours they had put in. Bartram refused – and the matter was sent to arbitration. Then in March there was a period of exceptionally bad weather, which kept the men from doing all outside work, though Bartram noted cynically that the weather seemed to be less of a problem at weekends when the men were working at overtime rates.

One of the issues that had plagued the industry in the pre-war years – and was to do so again – was the demarcation dispute. It had a long history, dating right back to the first introduction of the iron steamers that began to replace the old wooden sailing ships. A tradition had built up over the centuries, by which a boy began as an apprentice and gradually built up experience and skill until he had earned the proud title of shipwright. Now a new generation of workers had appeared in the yards: men who knew how to work with powerful engines and metal. It was not just that the shipwright was no longer automatically the highest paid member of the workforce, but they were also no longer necessarily the most important. The men from the older tradition fought hard to maintain their status and privileges, and one way in which this was done was by reaching agreements over which workers would be responsible for which particular job. A typical example came when a metal plate had to be fixed to a wooden frame: should the job go to the joiners who made things out of wood or to the metalworkers. It seems petty, but it led to a strike, which was only resolved when it was agreed that the metalworkers would drill the holes in the frame and the joiners would attach the wooden panels. Thanks, however, to the agreement reached between the government and the unions in the war years, strikes were banned and, for a while at least, time was not lost to such disputes. That did not mean, however, that all the problems that had existed between management and workers had totally disappeared. The particular nature of the industry made that impossible.

Traditionally, shipbuilding had been subjected to huge variations in demand that fluctuated with changing economic circumstances. When times were good, trade was good and more ships were ordered: when times were bad, orders dried up. One of the reasons that yards were reluctant to spend money on innovation was that in periods of slump, they had a lot of capital tied up in machinery that wasn't earning anything. It was easier and cheaper to hire a large workforce at comparatively low wages – and lay them off whenever the order book started to empty. Eustace d'Eyncourt, who had been so influential on the Landship Committee, was sympathetic when he looked back on his years on the Tyne and the Clyde:

Conditions of employment undoubtedly needed improving when I was young. It always struck me as particularly hard that such skilled, excellent and honest workmen as those I knew in the shipyards had to live in such a state of uncertainty and insecurity, having a good job at the moment but being entirely and helplessly dependent upon the variable conditions of trade … I realised to the full, when working among them how they all, especially the married men, had their future on their minds the whole time – not, as in my case, as something to look forward to, but with a sense of continued fear. From week to week any or all of them, however skilled, might at a week's notice, or even less, find themselves with only their savings to depend on.[5]

It was not even that straightforward: few of the families made enough to put any savings away, and d'Eyncourt himself recorded how it was common practice for the men to put on their best Sunday suits for church, and then pawn them to have enough cash to see them through to the next payday. It was not a situation that was likely to breed a sense of mutual trust and respect between the owners and the workers they employed. The different unions argued among themselves as well as with the management, while the tendency among most owners was to think of profits first, with any other considerations coming a long way second. There were a few shipyards that attempted to make sensible deals with the unions in the pre-war years, yet once hostilities started and agreements were made, everything changed. Like other industries, there were not only non-strike agreements but also agreements on dilution. Shipbuilding was no different, and women were soon employed in shipyards that had been exclusively male preserves, just as they were in many other industries. Mostly the changes went smoothly, but not everywhere, as we shall soon see.

Shipbuilding was clearly vital to the war effort and essential workers were given exemption from service in the armed forces. Viscount Pirrie, the man in charge of the mighty Harland & Wolff empire, which apart from its main yard in Belfast had subsidiaries in England and Scotland, used the system to get rid of 'troublemakers'.[6] All he had to do was declare their work non-essential and off they went to war. He was able to reorganise the whole workforce and rationalise production for maximum efficiency. In most yards, ships had been built to satisfy the customer's individual requirements, so that in effect each ship that left the yard was a one-off. Now, in wartime, there was an imperative to produce new vessels as quickly as possible. Pirrie began making a series of identical merchantmen, using standardised units and a certain amount of prefabrication – only made possible because of the new rules and regulations of wartime. But although it was easy for Pirrie at Harland & Wolff to get rid of men he didn't want, it proved rather more difficult for other shipyards to hold on to the men they needed.

Bartram's wartime diary told a story of frustrating arguments with the men from the ministry. By early 1916, the workforce had already been reduced from 750 to 480, yet he was being required to build patrol boats, a vital element in the fight against the German submarines. On 11 April an official arrived from the Ministry of Munitions wanting to call up more men, and he cast his eye on the riveters:

> He was doubtful about the rivet heaters & thought other boys could be set on; he had no idea that rivet heating required the services of men for much of the work but on hearing from Handford that this morning 2 rivet boys by stopping away from their work had kept 2 squads of riveters idle as others could not be got he did not touch them.[7]

Bartram's diary gives a fascinating glimpse into the wartime life of a moderately large shipyard. Like many others, when the war started they were switched from building merchant shipping to naval craft, but as the war progressed and the effects of the submarine war were felt, they were changed back again to the urgent task of building replacements for the sunken ships. They also experienced the war more directly. Being situated on the east coast at Sunderland they were well within the range of the Zeppelins. The first raid on the Wear took place on 1 April 1916. It only lasted about 15 minutes, and he recorded that although the works were not hit, they could hear the bombs exploding nearby. He said that he felt 'quite helpless', which indeed he was: Britain had yet to find an effective defence against air raids. The daughter of one of the platers was killed in the raid and his colleagues asked for time off for the funeral. Bartram refused, but much to his annoyance the men went anyway. There was not much he could do about that, either.

One of the conditions of the no-strike agreement was that disputes would be settled by arbitration. The shipyard workers, like all other industrial workers in those years, were faced with rapidly rising costs and felt they needed more pay to maintain a decent standard of living. Bartram's workforce was no exception: they put in a claim, management turned it down, and an academic was called in to settle the issue. The result was, according to Bartram, a 'monstrous injustice':

> The arbitrator was a Professor Irvine of Aberdeen, Professor of Law at Aberdeen University. He had not the remote idea of shipyard work, or terms or any of the usual ways that work is carried on between the men & employers. No doubt he did his best but he took the men's point of view. He refused to admit as evidence the figures put before him by Matthews as to what other yards were paying and seemed to have taken a dislike to Matthews.

It is perhaps not too surprising that the owners resented the intrusion of outsiders into their very closed world. In general, they had rather a low opinion of the men in Whitehall. Some years later, one yard produced its very own prayer intended to be said each morning by civil servants. It began:

> O Lord, grant this day that we come to no decisions, neither run into any kind of responsibility, and that all our doings be ordered to establish new departments from day unto day, and that we do always that which will make us sit tight. Grant, we beseech Thee that our duplicates and triplicates multiply fruitfully so that we, being defended from fear of insecurity, may pass our time (and the taxpayers' money) in rest and quietness.

No doubt it was very unfair to many hard-working people in the service, but it was a natural response that would have raised a laugh in most shipyards in Britain.

From the very start of the war the demand for warships escalated rapidly. Some yards, such as Bartram's, had to turn away from their more usual work to take on new challenges. Others had a long history of working for the navy. Scotts of Greenock had started making naval vessels at the beginning of the nineteenth century and had continued through from the age of sail to the age of steam. During the war years they built a wide variety of craft, including three battleships, three light cruisers and twelve destroyers. There were many technical advances. The destroyers, for example, still used steam power, but instead of coal Scotts used fuel oil for the boilers. As the war progressed, there was a steady increase in size and power that enabled the vessels to carry more armament and more fuel to increase their range. At the start of the war, Scotts' destroyers had engines producing 24,500 shaft horsepower, with a maximum speed of 29 knots: by 1918 the destroyers' turbines produced 44,000 shaft horsepower and had top speeds of 38 knots. These were gradual improvements, using well-tried technology. Now they faced a new challenge: they were to be among the first shipyards given the task of building submarines.

Submarine development had been going on for a long time. Surprisingly, there was an attempt at a submarine as early as 1620. It was based on the idea of filling a boat with so much ballast that it was almost totally submerged, but could still be rowed along. A trial on the Thames ended with a totally exhausted crew before the cumbersome vessel had made much headway. It was only in the nineteenth century, with the use of engines, that practical submarines came into use. But there was a problem: the Royal Navy was not quite sure how to use them. One school of thought saw them being used for harbour duty: another saw them as attack weapons working alongside the conventional battle fleet. The trouble with the latter idea was that in order to keep up with the fleet, the submarine had to travel at the same speed, and that requirement had a fundamental impact on design.

The first submarine built by Scotts was based not on a British design, but on one by Cesare Laurenti of Fiat San Giorgio of Italy. It had a double hull and was powered by a Fiat oil engine. Named simply S1, it was delivered to the navy at the outbreak of war. Because of the need for surface speed, the hull was boat shaped, instead of rounded, but even then could only manage 8.5 knots on the surface. Scotts set about solving the problem by abandoning the diesel engine and replacing it by steam turbines. Named *Swordfish*, the new vessel had two screws driven by a pair of turbines, but these were only to be used when high speed was essential for travelling on the surface. There was also an 800hp diesel engine, which had two functions: it worked a dynamo for recharging the submarine's batteries, and provided the main driving force at other times, including when the vessel was submerged.

Among the design problems was what to do with the funnel when the *Swordfish* dived. The answer was a complex system in which an electric motor pulled down the hinged funnel, and the space was capped off and made watertight using hydraulic gear. The *Swordfish* came closer to Admiralty requirements of moving at high speed, and it was claimed that it could reach 25 knots, though 20 knots seemed the most it ever managed in practice. Essentially the design was too complicated and, as it turned out, inherently dangerous.

Another steam submarine was developed at the Royal Naval Dockyard at Devonport, the K Class. Some idea of what those who worked on them and sailed in them thought of this particular vessel is obvious from their popular nickname: the 'Kalamity Kays'. K6 was submerged at the yard in what was supposed to be a quick trial of just a few minutes to make sure it could surface again without any problems: it remained under for two hours. The dockworkers, who had been trapped inside the hull uncertain when or even if they would be released, were understandably reluctant to take part in any further submarine trials. The various failures of the British submarine programme were not down to bad construction nor even bad design, but rather to the wrong questions being asked of the manufacturers.

It was the German submarine fleet, acting independently of other warships and hunting in packs undetected beneath the waves, that were almost to turn the whole course of the war. The British undoubtedly had the finest battle fleet in the world and if the war at sea had entirely depended on decisive sea battles they would have emerged triumphant. It did not.

It took some time for the Admiralty to admit that the most important thing that the shipyards could do to help the war effort was to ensure that they built merchantmen to replace those sunk by the U-boats. The precise figures are not clear, but it would seem that between 4,500 and 5,000 – and some authorities claim as many as 6,000 – ships were sunk. Britain relied heavily on imports of everything from the raw materials of industry to food for the population: without shipping replacements the war could have been lost. Shipbuilding was vital and the workers, on the whole, responded to the call just as others had done in other industries. It is all the more remarkable in that this was the industry that had been so plagued by demarcation disputes and was now throwing away the book, and not only allowing men to do work that would have been reserved for another trade, but even allowing women to undertake skilled work in the shipyards.

The waves of patriotic fervour that swept across the country engulfed most of the industry, but broke up on the banks of the Clyde. This was one area where opposition to the war was as fervent as approval of it was in the rest of the country, earning the area the title Red Clyde. It was not so much a matter of pacifism, as a belief that they were fighting the wrong enemy. According to *The Socialist* newspaper of February 1916: 'The class war is the only war worth waging.' Government propaganda urging men to join the forces was ubiquitous, but on the Clyde it was turned on its head. A famous poster showed an ashamed-looking man being asked by his little children, 'What did you do in the Great War, Daddy?' The Clydeside version had a typically top-hatted capitalist being asked the same question, and proudly answering: 'I did the workers'. A popular song made fun of the famous Kitchener poster:

Your King and Country Need You
Ye hardy sons of toil.
And will your King and Country need you
When they're sharing out the spoil?

The industry had suffered from bad relations between workers and employers for a very long time. Now both sides saw the outbreak of war as a chance to make big changes: for the employers it meant sweeping away restrictive practices; for the men it was an opportunity to raise their living standards. As it was clear that living costs were rising, the shop stewards put in for a claim of an extra 2*d* per hour in 1914; the employers responded by offering three farthings – the farthing was one-quarter of a penny. Elsewhere such claims were met by arbitration, but in Glasgow, although no strike was called, there was a ban on overtime. One of the employers was Sir William Weir, whose company made pumps and other equipment for the Admiralty. He had also gone into shell production at the start of the war, declaring that any profit he made from that side of his business would be donated to the Red Cross. He was outraged by the industrial action:

> Every hour lost by a workman which COULD HAVE been worked, HAS been worked by a German workman, who in that time has produced, say, an additional shell … to kill the British workman's brother-in-arms, or perhaps a bomb to be dropped on his wife and children.[8]

Weir brought matters to a head when he brought in skilled fitters and turners from America, and word soon spread that they were being paid 6*s* per week more than their British counterparts. William Gallacher, a shop steward at the Albion motor works in Glasgow, who was later to become one of Britain's few communist members of Parliament, promptly called the workforce there out on strike in sympathy. Trade unions were barred from striking under the Defence of the Realm Act, so an unofficial 'Labour With-holding Committee' was set up, with Gallacher as chairman. By now, the strike was seen as primarily about pay, rather than politics, and when it went to a ballot of the workforce, the vote in favour of staying on strike was overwhelming, 6,439 to 594, in spite of vehement opposition in the press. The strikers were denounced as unpatriotic and Gallacher described as 'a drunken blaggard'. Just as the socialist press had produced cartoons of wicked capitalists, the newspapers of Glasgow responded by showing, for example, a striking shipyard worker stabbing a British soldier in the back. After three weeks, the employers increased their offer to 1*d* per hour, not exactly a vast increase over the three farthings offered earlier, but a face-saver for all concerned. It was also a great relief to the strikers' families, as there was no strike pay available as this was an unofficial stoppage. It did not bring industrial peace to the Clyde.

The strike was over, but a new organisation appeared to take on the role of the Labour With-holding Committee – the Clyde Workers' Committee, with Gallacher in the chair and a very active membership, among whom David Kirkwood played a prominent part. He was a shop steward convener at the Parkhead Forge, part of the William Beardmore company, among the leading manufacturers in naval construction work. Their first challenge came in November 1915, when there were sharp rises in rents in the Glasgow area, most being well over 10 per cent. This resulted in a rent strike by a number of tenants, who were taken to the Small Debts Court. The court was used to settling small claims, quietly and unobtrusively, but on this occasion a crowd of some 15,000 workers gathered outside and a deputation went in to tell the sheriff that if he made an order for payment, there would be a mass walk-out. No order was made and the government announced that it was about to freeze rents to the 1914 level to prevent profiteering. It was a famous victory for the strikers, and although the committee claimed most of the credit, it seems to have been a spontaneous response, born out of a far more general sense of repulsion among the workers. Housing conditions were notoriously bad, and to be asked to pay more while their pay was being pegged in the name of patriotism and the war effort, was more than many could stomach.

A far more serious situation rose when the trade unions agreed on the Munitions of War Act 1915. The workers' committee issued a statement, addressed to 'all Clyde workers', in which they voiced their total opposition to the act in fiery language: 'The support given to the Munitions Act by the officials was an Act of Treachery to the Working Class.' They vowed to fight for the repeal of 'all the pernicious legislation that has recently been imposed upon us'. One of the first sections of the government act to be fiercely opposed was the one that restricted workers from leaving one job for another without permission. As Kirkwood put it, the act had 'bound the workers to Beardmore as completely as if it had branded "B" on their brows'. Attempts by Lloyd George to assert his charismatic magic failed to appease the militants. Though that particular section of the act was soon to be dropped, a far more bitter battle was about to be fought over dilution: the trade union leaders had all agreed to it, but not the Clyde Workers' Committee.

The rule of the militants was short-lived. There were many in the shipyards and the factories on both sides of the conflict who were ready to compromise. Dilution was taking place, and many of the new workers coming into the industry were women whose husbands were serving in France and who were badly in need of the extra income. Management had learned the lesson that it was better to try carrots than sticks, and began consultation processes with some of the more moderate union leaders. There was not the same groundswell of support for strike action. Under the Defence of the Realm Act, the authorities now felt confident enough to arrest Gallacher and the other signatories to the original document for inciting industrial action. There was a strike in support of the leader, but when he was granted bail it simply fizzled out. Next in the management's sights was Kirkwood, who had his privileges as the convener of the shop stewards revoked. Again there was a strike, but there was no real attempt to spread it to other yards and factories, and that in turn collapsed. It was clear that the Clyde Workers' Committee was not the force it had been. Gallacher came up for trial in Edinburgh and was sentenced to a year in jail, and other committee members were sentenced to various prison terms running from three months to three years.

The years of Red Clyde came to an end, symbolically if not actually, in June 1917 when Lloyd George, the arch enemy of the movement and the man who had introduced the Munitions Act, was given the freedom of the city of Glasgow. It had seemed for a time that the Clyde Workers' Committee could have a serious effect on the shipbuilding industry. In the event, they managed to help get some small improvements in wages and a freezing of rents, real gains for the workforce, but such gains had been acquired elsewhere in other industries – and in other shipyards in Britain – without the revolutionary fervour. For the vast majority in the industry, work went forward without serious interruption and was of huge importance. Throughout the war years one of Britain's oldest industries was forced to make some changes in order to meet the huge demands for both navy and merchant shipping, but essentially the technology did not move forward very rapidly. The same could not be said about the next construction industry we will look at: flight. In fact, at the start of the war there could scarcely be said to be an industry at all. Suddenly Britain was taking to the skies.

12

THE FLIGHT PIONEERS

The military took to the skies long before the invention of the aeroplane. The Montgolfier brothers gave their first public demonstration of a hot-air balloon in 1783 and its potential for military use was realised at once. Benjamin Franklin wrote in that same year of the advantage of a balloon 'for elevating an Engineer to take a view of an Enemy's Army, Works, &c; conveying intelligence into, or out of, a besieged Town, giving Signals to Distant Places, or the like'.[1] The idea was soon taken up in France, and the world's first military balloon, not a hot-air balloon but one filled with hydrogen, was used for observation by the French Army at the Battle of Fleurus in 1794, during the Revolutionary War. The value of balloons, particularly for guiding artillery, became appreciated more and more over the years.

During the American Civil War, balloons were fitted with electric telegraphs that enabled the balloonists to report enemy movements to the ground with great efficiency. A British officer, Captain F. Beaumont, was attached to the American Unionist Balloon Corps and returned to England full of enthusiasm for the idea. From 1862 to 1873 he badgered the British Army generals to experiment with observation balloons. He gave demonstrations but the military showed their all too common distaste for innovation. He eventually gave up the fight. Then in 1878 the Royal Aircraft Establishment was formed as a part of the army under the auspices of the Royal Engineers. Its first head was Captain James Templar, a keen amateur balloonist, who arrived at Woolwich, bringing his own balloon with him. The following year Britain had its first balloon observation corps in training and set up a research establishment looking into different aspects of balloon manufacture. At first, a great deal of attention was given to how to make hydrogen efficiently and how to use it. One important technical advance was made: the use of hydrogen compressed in cylinders to keep the balloon inflated. Another area of interest was the balloon envelope. It was Templar who discovered that goldbeater's skin, a form of parchment used in the manufacture of gold leaf, was the ideal material. This was actually made from the large intestine of the calf, and any individual piece was never more than 2ft square. The job of preparing the skins at the balloon factory and stitching them together was mostly the work of women, the earliest example of women working in the aviation industry.

A technique was developed for working with observation balloons. The balloons were allowed to rise to a height of 1,000–2,000ft at the end of a steel cable. The cable itself was controlled from a winch mounted on a wagon hauled by a team of horses, or, in the case of the various African campaigns of the late nineteenth century, by bullocks. There was, however, always a problem with stability with the tethered balloons, and experiments were made with large box kites to lift the observational balloons off the ground. They were not entirely successful but in 1896 two German officers combined a dirigible balloon with a box kite that proved remarkably stable. It was the forerunner of the observation balloons that would be used by the British Army in the First World War. It had taken a while, but the British military were finally airborne.

At first, the use of ballooning by the military was strictly limited to observation, but other ideas had been around since ballooning began. Benjamin Franklin, who had been an enthusiast for the military use of balloons from the first, had also had a far more ambitious idea. He envisaged a task force of 5,000 balloons, each carrying two soldiers:

'and where is the prince who can afford so to cover his Country with Troops for its Defense, as that Ten Thousand men descending from the Clouds might not in many places do an infinite amount of mischief before a Force could be brought together to repel them?' The problem with that idea was that at this stage of development balloons went where the wind blew them, with no means of control. I have my own vivid recollections of a balloon flight from the Thames valley where, rather alarmingly, our flight path was taking us directly over the missile silos at what was then the heavily defended American base at Greenham Common. It was deemed wiser to land first, even if we did end up in a field full of inquisitive bullocks. Franklin's 10,000 men could have been taken on a similarly disastrous route.

For a balloon to be steered it needed to have some sort of power, and the first successful model didn't appear until 1850 when a French clockmaker, Pierre Jullien, built a model of a balloon with a gondola underneath, on which were mounted two propellers powered by clockwork. It inspired Henri Giffard to design his own full-scale version, with a small steam engine and propeller, in which he made his first flight in 1852. The age of the airship had begun. There were two basic variations. The dirigible consisted of a single envelope that kept its shape due to the pressure of the gas that filled it. The alternative was the rigid-framed airship that was famously developed in Germany by Ferdinand von Zeppelin. He began his career as an army officer and, like Captain Beaumont, he was given permission to go to America to see what was happening in the American Civil War. It was during his American tour that he made his first balloon ascent. The latter part of the nineteenth century was an exciting time for aviation developments in Germany. Otto Lilienthal was making experimental flights using gliders, including a biplane, and had demonstrated how it was possible to control such a craft in the air. Zeppelin was impressed, but felt that the immediate future was better served by lighter-than-air craft and after leaving the army began to develop his own ideas of airship design. In 1898 he took out a patent for a long cylindrical airship with a rigid frame, which was kept aloft by a number of hydrogen-filled bags within the skeleton. He worked with Daimler to adapt the new internal combustion engines and to improve on the Maybach petrol engine used to power the first craft. Within a decade the Zeppelins were beginning to offer passenger flights, linking a number of German cities, and by 1913 the first passenger airship had made over 700 flights in the year, with over 1,000 hours of flying time.[2] More importantly, as far as the immediate future was concerned, the German Navy had acquired its first Zeppelin in 1912.

The British Army showed no great interest in airships, being quite content with its observational balloons, so it was left to the navy to react to what Zeppelin was doing in Germany. Britain had already built dirigibles, but it was felt that the time had come to investigate rigid-framed airships. The first contract went to Vickers in 1909, who agreed to undertake the construction and to build a special shed at their base at Barrow-in-Furness in which to do the work. But they insisted as part of the deal that they were given a ten-year monopoly on airship construction for the navy. The design was to be the joint responsibility of Lieutenant Usborne of the Admiralty and C.G. Robertson of Vickers. The official designation was HMA1, though it was to be popularly known as the *Mayfly*, largely based on the early Zeppelins but containing one novel feature: mooring equipment in the nose that enabled it to be attached to a mast.

The construction shed was built next to an existing dock, and the ship was to be built on a floating platform. The idea was that it could easily be floated in and out for trials. In the event, the air trials were never to take place. On 24 September 1911 the *Mayfly* was floated out of the dock, but before the whole ship had emerged from the shed it was caught by a violent gust of wind. With half the vessel held within the narrow shed and the front half blown by the wind, Britain's first rigid airship broke in two. At this point the Admiralty more or less lost interest. Vickers abandoned construction.

In 1913 a new department was set up to investigate the idea again, and among the engineers taking part in the design this time was a young Barnes Wallis, later to become famous for his dam-busting, bouncing bomb. Churchill was unenthusiastic, but agreed to see a demonstration at a site near the mouth of the Medway. The craft was

Airship No. 3, *Astra*. Usborne, now a lieutenant commander, took it on himself to pilot the craft from Farnborough to a rendezvous with the Admiralty yacht, together with a young officer recently attached to the naval wing, T.R. Cave-Browne-Cave, who was later to give his own account of the flight. It is worth quoting at some length as it gives a very good idea of just how hazardous early flights were and how primitive the navigational techniques that were available:

At dawn of the great day there was dense fog. We left Farnborough in *Astra* at about 6.30 a.m. with the intention of following the Southern Railway to London and then the river to Grain at the mouth of the Medway. The fog was so thick that we could see the railway only at intervals. We spotted a station at which the line was crossed by a large road. Was it Wimbledon or, as Usborne thought, Sutton? He turned North to find the river and immediately looking slightly upwards, we saw a tree which must have been on Wimbledon Common. Then we found the river. There was still dense fog and the next thing we saw was the water tower on Shooter's Hill. From this definite fix, Usborne set course for Chatham where the shape of the river is distinctive. By the greatest good luck we got a sight of the foundations of the new airship shed being built at Kingsnorth halfway between Chatham and Sheerness. This was quite unique. The time was 9.30 a.m. which gave us 30 mins in which to do nine miles to Grain. We saw Kingsnorth long enough to make a reliable estimate of windspeed and direction. Usborne, therefore, decided to fly very slowly and silently to a point, slightly to windward of Grain, from which he would drift in complete silence. We could see nothing at 10 a.m. so Usborne made, by the bellows fog horn, the code signal asking permission to anchor. We were so close to the party waiting for us that the reply came at once by word of mouth – 'Anchor immediately'. We let go the trail rope which was 300 ft long, the end reached the ground and was found by the landing party who hauled us down.[3]

Having been an air navigator once myself I can scarcely imagine what it must have been like blundering around the sky, virtually blind, and without the benefit of any modern instruments. I can also only admire the skill of hitting their rendezvous on time. It was a hugely impressive performance – and certainly impressed Churchill, which was the whole object of the exercise. It did mean that when war came there was an airship programme under way. Vickers now went back into production with the R9. This was a big airship, 562ft long and 53ft in diameter, held aloft by seventeen gas bags with a total capacity of 890,000 cubic feet. Power was supplied by four 180hp Maybach engines, built by the motor manufacturer Wolseley, giving a top speed of 45mph. The first trial flight was made in November 1916 and the airship only entered service with the Admiralty in March 1917. Compared with Germany, Britain made very little use of airships during the war. Germany built far more airships – by the time the Royal Navy had accepted its first rigid airship, the German Navy had acquired more than seventy. Not only had they more craft, but they were far more advanced. By the end of the war the Zeppelins were able to reach speeds of 80mph and operate at heights up to 26,200ft.

The development of the airship in Britain was comparatively slow and, in terms of manufacturing, comparatively unimportant. The same could not be said of the story of the heavier-than-air craft, the aeroplane. In fact, the speed of development was quite simply extraordinary, and to understand just how exceptional it was you have to look at what was happening in the few years immediately before the outbreak of war.

Experimental work on aircraft really began with Sir George Cayley, a wealthy landowner and an enthusiastic amateur engineer, who wrote a paper on the principles of powered flight that was published in *Nicholson's Journal* 1809–10. He went further than that and built a number of experimental gliders in one of which a boy was 'floated off the ground for several yards'. In his work he established several of the fundamentals necessary for flight, including the fixed, cambered wing to provide lift, an airscrew for propulsion and a fixed vertical tail for directional stability. The one thing that held him back was the lack of a suitable source of power. He realised, however, that it needed more than one individual working alone to conquer the air. 'I think it is a national disgrace not to realise by public subscription the proper scientific experiments, necessarily too expensive for any private purse, which could ensure in this country the glory of being the first to establish the navigation of the dry universal ocean of the terrestrial atmosphere.'[4] It was to be half a century before the Royal Aeronautical Society was formed in 1866. There were numerous other advances in aircraft design, including the development of elevators and other devices by the German inventor Otto Lilienthal. But Britain was not destined to gain the glory of being the first to achieve a flight in a powered plane that Cayley had hoped for. That honour was to go to two American brothers.

In fact, the famous first manned powered flight by a heavier-than-air craft built by Orville and Wilbur Wright on 17 December 1903 attracted very little attention at first, largely because the Wrights wanted to keep their work secret at this early stage of development. It was not perhaps the most spectacular flight ever made: more of a hop of a few yards, lasting just twelve seconds. The basic biplane design was based on ideas first developed by Lilienthal. Although the Wright brothers' success owed a great deal to other early experimenters with flying machines, they also had a background that helped them find the right materials for the job. They had their own bicycle repair shop and were accustomed to working with tubular metal frames that combined light weight with strength. They were also able to take advantage of the other new developments in road transport, with a petrol engine for power. These were two of the essential features: a light frame and a lightweight, but powerful, engine. The airscrews were situated at the back of the plane, pushing it along, unlike later planes where the airscrews were at the front, pulling it. Both systems were used in early planes: pusher and tractor airscrews.

In order to get enough speed to get airborne, the Wright brothers' plane was fitted with skids and launched down a ramp, much as a modern ski jumper achieves his brief flight. The pilot lay on his stomach to manage the controls. It used wing warping for lateral control, but had no tail. Instead there was a front elevator. It was actually very difficult to manage. Visitors to the excellent Swiss Museum of Transport in Lucerne can try out their own skills on a Wright flight simulator: I have to confess I crashed soon after taking off on my virtual flight. The Wrights built two more craft and by 1905 they had a practical machine that could follow a circular course, and they stayed aloft for over half an hour. Then they simply stopped flying for three years. It was only in 1908 that the world became aware of their achievement. The dates are important to bear in mind. Europeans were not aware of what had been achieved until just six years before the start of the war, yet over those few years a major industry would be born.

The next major advance came from France, where Louis Blériot had been working on flying machines of one sort or another since the beginning of the century, including an ornithoptor, which it was hoped would literally fly like a bird by flapping its wings. It was never going to work, but he continued with his plans and in 1903 joined with another pioneer, Gabriel Voisin, to form what was almost certainly the world's first aircraft construction company, though their first efforts were limited to building gliders. The partnership did not last but Blériot continued developing his own ideas, which varied from the box-kite type of design used by the Wrights to a canard, a monoplane with the tail at the front, before eventually settling on a monoplane with the tail where tails would normally be found in nature – at the back. The Blériot XI can reasonably be described as the first modern aeroplane, and the inventor decided to use it to try and win the £1,000 prize offered by the English newspaper the *Daily Mail* for anyone who could fly across the English Channel. He succeeded in 1909 in a flight lasting just over half an hour. He was now in a position to begin manufacturing aircraft, some of which found purchasers in Britain who were to use the flying experience they gained in Blériots to begin work on designing and making machines of their own.

The first attempt at powered flight in Britain appears to have taken place at the then new motor racing circuit at Brooklands, destined to play an important role as the site of the country's first flying school.

The would-be aviator was a Frenchman, M. Bellamy, who arrived either in late 1906 or early 1907 with a machine described as 'a great white bird', which was quite apt as photos show bird-like wings and it had a tail that flapped up and down. The first attempt was made with the machine fitted with floats so that it could take off from a lake, but it hit an obstruction and sank. It was then rebuilt and fitted with wheels but never left the ground. The disgruntled Frenchman explained that the air in Britain was obviously different from the air in France and took his bird back to the better atmosphere. The next would-be aviator was a most remarkable character, an American Samuel Franklin Cody.

Cody's real name was Cowdery, but he changed it when he began his career as a showman – describing himself as a 'sharp shooter and Cowboy'. It was no accident that the new surname was the same as that of the spectacularly successful stager of Wild West shows, Buffalo Bill Cody. He even looked like Buffalo Bill, wearing similar clothes and sporting the same goatee beard. He brought his own show to Britain but soon discovered that there was an even bigger market for western melodramas, with himself in the starring role. His most successful production was *The Klondike Nugget*, which earned him enough money to indulge his hobby, designing and flying massive kites. He soon put his hobby to good use by arranging flying demonstrations during the day while performing his melodrama in the evening.

At the outbreak of the Boer War, Cody wrote to the War Office to offer his services in designing man-carrying kites for observation. His offer was taken seriously and he eventually found himself with an official position in charge of construction and training for kites at the newly established aeronautical centre at Farnborough. He began work at the army balloon factory in 1903 and was soon experimenting with an even bolder idea: a powered kite. His first effort was flown without anyone on board and tethered to a steel cable, but it encouraged Cody to take the next obvious step to convert his powered aeroplane into one that could carry a man in free flight. He ordered an Antoinette engine from France and built his first plane in the airship hangar at Farnborough.

An artist's impression of the devastation caused to British merchantmen by the German U-boat campaign.

The bombardment of the seaside resort of Scarborough by the German Navy caused outrage, not least because there were no strategic targets, just ordinary houses such as these.

Volunteers serving refreshments to servicemen at Victoria Station.

A rather lurid representation of a train being attacked by a Zeppelin.

Women took on many railway jobs, including carriage cleaning.

Soldiers being trained
in boat handling on
the Basingstoke Canal.
(Michael E. Ware)

Women played a vital
role in keeping essential
services running.
Pictured here is a
London bus conductor.

Women signing up for work in munitions factories.

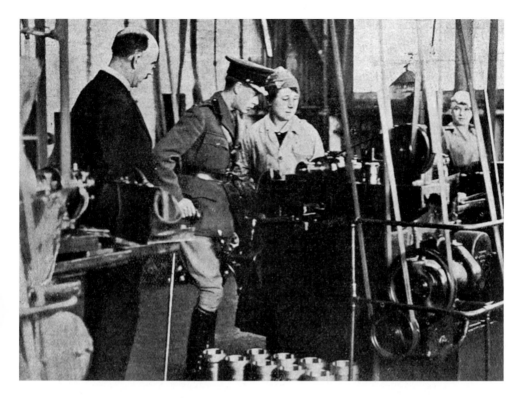

The Prince of Wales
inspecting the work of
women in a munitions
factory.

This drawing by Joseph
Pennell gives a good idea
of the scale of work in an
armaments factory.

Putting up a notice in a pub to remind customers that it was now against the law to buy a drink for a friend: a government measure designed to reduce drunkenness.

A variety of private cars and vans requisitioned by the army at the start of the war.

'WOLSELEY'

WE shall be pleased to add your order to our Waiting List, for delivery when this becomes possible.

WOLSELEY MOTORS, Limited, BIRMINGHAM.
Proprietors, VICKERS Limited.

An advert for a car that would probably not be available until after the war.

With no petrol available for private motoring, bags filled with town gas were strapped on top of vehicles as fuel.

Tanks in action: with their ability to cover the roughest ground they were to prove decisively effective weapons.

Shipbuilding in wartime was still being carried out in open berths as it had been in the nineteenth century.

Women in the shipbuilding industry on the Clyde proved themselves capable of working with precision machinery. (Business Records Centre, University of Glasgow)

Samuel Franklin Cody at the controls of Britain's very first military aircraft.

An array of steam hammers at the Alexander Stephens shipyard on the Clyde. (Scottish Maritime Museum)

Winston Churchill, then First Lord of the Admiralty, inspecting a seaplane.

Women at work in an aeroplane factory.

A posed photograph of miners working a moderately
high seam of coal.

Soldiers receiving instruction on ploughing with an American Titan tractor.

Weavers at work in a Gloucestershire woollen mill, using power looms driven by belt and line shafting. (Stroudwater Textile Trust)

Women's Land Army volunteers showing their skills in a recruitment campaign.

Digging for Victory: a family turning over wasteland to grow vegetables.

On 19 September 1907 British Army Aeroplane No. 1 took to the skies, flying the Union Jack from a pole fixed to the fuselage and with Cody at the controls. Twenty-seven seconds into the flight, Cody had to make a steeply banked turn to avoid some trees, a wing tip hit the ground and Britain's first successful flight by a piloted aeroplane was at an end. Undeterred, Cody at once began on a new, improved model. By now, however, the army, never very keen on novelty, had decided that aeroplanes were a waste of time and that they should spend all their resources on airships and balloons. Cody lost his job and his backing, but he was allowed to keep his plane. He went on to develop more sophisticated versions and now had a new dream: to build a 'flying omnibus' or, as we more prosaically would call it, an airliner. He began giving passenger flights and it was on one of these excursions that his plane crashed, killing both him and his passenger in August 1913.

The failure of the army to follow up on the first experiments at Farnborough meant that the development of aviation in Britain was left to others. What is so fascinating about this part of aviation history is that we have now reached 1907 with Britain's first powered flight by a heavier-than-air plane and, although there had been greater advances in Europe and America, the machines in use in Britain were still quite primitive. Yet Britain would be fighting a war in the air in just seven years. The advances that were made in that very short time were not down to the military establishment, nor even powerful companies in most cases, but depended to an extraordinary extent on the willingness of enthusiasts to risk their own money – and their lives – in experiments with this infant craft. It was not yet in a state where it could be described as an industry. The pioneers came from a variety of backgrounds and had aeronautical careers with, literally, many ups and downs. It was from the work of these men that the industry that would provide the machines of war would evolve.[5]

Like the Wright brothers, many of the pioneers came from a background in transport, especially in cycling. Charles Stewart Rolls, whose name was to become famous as half of Rolls Royce, read science at Cambridge and took up cycle racing as a hobby. John Siddeley was a member of the Anfield Bicycle Club and, on a machine of his own design, was the first to cycle from Land's End to John o'Groats, and would gradually move from motor manufacturing to aircraft building. Alliott Verdon Roe was an apprentice at the Lancashire & Yorkshire Locomotive Works, and supplemented his income by competing in cycle races for prize money. The list can be continued, but what they all had in common was an interest in what was then the latest thing in transport innovation. Interestingly, the bicycle was among the first vehicles to be motorised when Daimler created the first motorbike. The essence of the motorbike was a light frame and comparatively light engine: exactly what was needed in aviation.

The career of A.V. Roe was typical in some ways to that of many other of the pioneers in the sense that everything he did grew out of a personal enthusiasm. He was educated at King's College, London and left to take up a job as a ship's engineer with the British & South African Royal Mail Company. It is said that his inspiration came when he was watching the seemingly effortless gliding of the albatross on its long ocean journeys. He left the sea to work in the motor industry but spent his spare time making flying models. It was when he heard about the Wright brother's flight that he began to see that this was a potential career. He was keen to propagate his ideas, and wrote a lengthy article for the engineering supplement of *The Times* in 1906. It was published, but with the addition of a note from the editor:

> It is not to be supposed that we in any way adopt the writer's estimate of his undertaking, being of the opinion, indeed, that all attempts at artificial aviation are not only dangerous to human life, but foredoomed to failure from the engineering standpoint.[6]

This ranks as one of the all-time least successful professional assessments of an idea.

The opinion did not deter Roe, who wrote to the Wright brothers offering his services as their European agent. They were already busy trying to sell their designs to various government bodies and turned him down. He next wrote to the newly formed Aero Club asking for and getting a job as unpaid secretary. His only income came when he entered a model aircraft competition in 1907, with a model powered by an elastic band, and won the first prize of £75. The resulting exhibition attracted a lot of attention, but no one seemed very interested in turning models into full-sized planes. A colonel from the Royal Engineers balloon factory merely noted: 'we have learned very little from the machines exhibited'. There seemed to be no possibility of receiving any official or commercial backing for his ideas. He went ahead anyway and built a new model, with the help of a local cycle shop, and fitted a 9hp motorcycle engine to his plane. It was given trials at the newly opened Brooklands motor circuit. Again, success in the air received little encouragement from potential backers. But at least Roe's brother was impressed and, as head of a successful manufacturing company in Manchester, was able to do something about it. He helped set up A.V. Roe and Co. and the inventor finally had the means to put his ideas into practice.

From the new premises in Manchester, Roe soon started producing extraordinarily advanced designs. In 1911 he produced the first plane to have an enclosed cockpit, and the following year he gave demonstrations to the military. In October 1912 he created a new record for long-distance flight of seven and a half hours – just five years after the first British flight of less than half a minute. In 1913 he built the Avro 504 and, if anything showed how far aviation had travelled in a short time, this plane did the task. It was powered by a Gnome Lambda engine, designed in France, which had its seven cylinders arranged in a circle and, whereas his original motorcycle engine had produced a modest 9hp, the new engine gave an impressive 76.5hp. Anyone thinking of First World War aircraft probably has an image of the Avro in mind. It was a biplane with a closed-in fuselage, unlike the skeletal frames of older planes, with the conventional tractor propeller in the nose. A few were ordered for the military, but once the war began it was to prove its worth. It had two distinctions to its name: the first plane to carry out a bombing raid on Germany and the less welcome one of being the first British plane to be shot down. Once it went into production, the flow never stopped.

The engines were built under licence by Daimler at Coventry and the majority of the planes were built in Roe's own factory. Altogether an astonishing 8,790 Avro 504s were built between 1914 and 1918. Apart from its use as a fighting aircraft it also became the standard machine for training young pilots.

The Avro was a huge improvement over earlier planes used for pilot training. In the early years of the war, the Maurice Farman Shorthorn, built in France and known to those who flew it as 'Rumpity', was widely used. It was a pusher biplane and, like other early planes, had an open bodywork and wings supported by a web of wires and struts. One of those who learned to fly in one of these machines was a young W.E. Johns, later to be famous as author of the Biggles books. He was not very impressed. 'I learnt to fly in an old Rumpity, which would as soon go one way as another. You had to use both hands, both feet and your teeth to keep it going where you wanted to go.'[7] And in one of the Biggles stories, an instructor gave this advice to a young pilot learning to fly a Rumpity: 'The easiest way to find out if all the wires are in their place is to put a canary between the wings; if the bird gets out you know there is a wire missing somewhere.'

When looking at the efforts being made to manufacture planes during the war years, it is always as well to remember that this was an infant industry, making things up as it went along, with no real basis in scientific or even aeronautical engineering theory. So it is not surprising to find that the training period for young pilots could be as dangerous as combat, with a combination of untried planes and wholly inexperienced pilots. Johns' own first solo flight was recorded in the log: 'Time in air: five seconds. Height: 30 feet. Remarks: crashed taking off.' He was more fortunate than his roommate, Tony. They shared the same machine for practice flights, tossing a coin to see who would go up. One day Tony won: 'At 2,000 feet it shed a wing and spun into the ground with all the ferocity the type could display when it was out of humour. It took the mechanics most of the day to dig Tony out, so I heard.' This accident was due to some sort of structural failure, but in other cases, the young trainees were sent up almost at once on solo flights and simply lacked the knowledge and judgement to cope with any sort of emergency. It was said that pilots were safer flying in combat than they were in training.

The men who designed and built the first planes had similar dangers to face. Hessell Tiltman was taken on as an engineer by De Havilland and he was responsible, among other things, for calculating stresses and specifying standards that had to be met:

> Having been responsible for many of the stress calculations and knowing only too well some of their limitations, I was, as the observer, often very frightened particularly with Gathergood who always threw all machines about the sky in a most alarming manner. When coming out of what appeared to feel like a terminal dive, I often wished I had specified a ¼ in. bolt instead of a 2 BA.[8]

Those who flew the aircraft were often equally dubious about what the designers had produced. One officer asked to report on the effectiveness of a recently designed bombsight chose what he considered the safest spot from which to record the results: the centre of the target. Those responsible for ordering the planes in the first place were often even more sceptical. A newly appointed director at the Admiralty Air Department in 1915 came to look at blueprints for a new seaplane, being prepared by the designer:

> I explained my concern with the project and then, after looking at the prints for a minute or two, he asked, 'Where are the sails?' It took a moment or two to realise that the wings were indicated and I then explained the drawings in more detail. Then, 'Will it fly?' and I said 'yes' to get the response, 'It's all very well for you to tell me that it *will* fly but I was down at Grain recently and saw a machine that looked like this one careering across the water like a – duck with its wing shot away.'[9]

These are just a few of the examples of the problems faced by the designers of planes and those who had to learn how to fly them during the war years. There were at least as many problems, and dangers, that had to be faced by the pre-war pioneers. Charles Rolls was the most famous early casualty. He had enthusiastically embraced all forms of modern transport, starting with the bicycle and moving into cars, when he moved into partnership with Henry Royce. He was an enthusiastic balloonist and it was an obvious next step to move on to aeroplanes. He was wealthy enough to buy a Wright aircraft for himself and tried to persuade the company to go into aircraft manufacture: he was turned down. Rolls Royce was to become among the best known of aero engine builders, but Rolls did not live to see it. He died in a plane crash in 1910.

Most of the pioneers made their own way into aviation. One of the great names associated with the fighting planes of the war was that of Frederick Handley Page. He had originally trained as an electrical engineer at Finsbury Technical College, but he was soon enthused by aviation and joined the newly formed Aero Club. There he met a Parisian, José Weiss, who was one of the few of the early designers who had made a study of the infant science of aerodynamics. Weiss had been working with ideas for gliders and they began building a machine using materials 'borrowed' from Handley Page's company. In 1908 Handley Page felt confident enough to start his own aircraft construction company near Dagenham. The factory was actually no more than a series of wooden huts on a piece of wasteland near Barking Creek. His first monoplane had handlebars to control the elevators and a foot bar for the rudder. It made its first flight and promptly crashed. The one thing that could be said about the early planes was that they were slow and seldom got high off the ground before coming to grief. The inventor simply brushed himself down, collected the pieces and started again. There were to be many more experiments before they arrived at the Type E, another monoplane with crescent-shaped wings, designed by Weiss, and a Gnome engine. In 1912 Handley Page flew it down to Brooklands, making the very first aeroplane flight over London. He managed to get a government order but the operation was still being run with almost no capital. When an official inspector arrived to see how work was progressing, he could only locate 1 per cent of the parts needed to complete the job.

The early monoplanes were notable more for their crashes than their flights, and the government decreed that in future they would only order biplanes. The Admiralty turned out to be rather keener then the army on ordering planes of any sort, partly because Churchill, the First Sea Lord, was an enthusiast. By now Handley Page had also turned to biplane design and he received a request from Commander Murray F. Sueter for a twin-engined bomber capable of attacking naval and Zeppelin bases. The first version was modestly sized, and did not thrill the commander: 'What I want is a bloody paralyser, not a toy.'[10] It wasn't until 1915 that the first successful Handley Page bomber went into production, a monster for its time with a 100ft wing span and powered by Rolls Royce engines producing 320hp, and able to carry sixteen 112lb bombs. It was a genuine paralyser. The company went on to manufacture improved versions that were the most successful bombers of the war.

The other company that can lay claim to be the first to go into manufacturing full time was started by the Short brothers. They also offered planes to the Admiralty and they were to specialise in seaplanes. When the first were delivered they were considered so dangerous that the Admiralty asked for four volunteers to fly them, who had to be unmarried: they didn't want to be blamed for creating young widows. In the event, 200 men volunteered. In 1912 a Short plane flew off a special platform constructed on HMS *Africa*, making it the world's first aircraft carrier. Similar stories of other pioneers could be repeated, men such as Tommy Sopwith whose name would always be remembered for the famous Sopwith Camel. But not all the first aircraft were born out of the enthusiasm of individuals, who got into building aircraft simply because they had first come to love flying.

George Holt Thomas was the son of the owner of the *Daily Graphic* a newspaper that had supported the early adventurers and given them publicity.[11] He talked to the leading figures of the day and realised that there were commercial opportunities. He obtained a licence to market the Farman aircraft in Britain and another to sell the French rotary Gnome engines. Encouraged by this success he decided to start manufacturing, but lacked the necessary technical expertise. Hugh Borroughes of the Farnborough Balloon Factory had already helped by translating the Farman and Gnome technical manuals into English so he was an obvious choice for the job of general manager of the new Aircraft Manufacturing Company. Another of his acquaintances, Geoffrey De Havilland, had been designer and test pilot at Farnborough, but he had been moved over to a new, duller job as aircraft inspector. He enthusiastically accepted the role of chief designer, helped by a handsome salary of £600 per year plus commission on any aircraft he designed. He had hardly had a chance to start work before war was declared and he was promptly called up. Fortunately someone soon recognised that he would be rather more valuable designing aircraft than flying them, and he returned to the company with the rank of captain.

It soon became apparent that in order to meet the demands of war, the company needed new premises. At this stage there were two main types of frame: the tubular steel derived from the bicycle industry, and wood. It was decided to look for a company that had a high reputation for first-rate carpentry. They found just what they were looking for in the unlikeliest of surroundings, with H.H. Martyn & Co., of Cheltenham, whose speciality was producing intricate decoration for elegant stately homes, working with anything from plaster to timber. The two companies eventually merged to form the Gloucestershire Aircraft Company, and the fashionable spa had a new industry. To increase production, they also moved into the magnificent glass-domed Victorian Winter Gardens, an entertainment venue next to the town hall. It must have been the most bizarre aircraft factory of all time. Ironically, the factory established to make planes to bomb Germany was itself destroyed by the Luftwaffe in the Second World War.

Much of aircraft construction at this period, particularly the construction of the basic frames, hardly called for the high skills in carpentry possessed by the Cheltenham craftsmen. The one exception was the making of propellers. As the industry progressed and aeronautical design became more sophisticated so the standards required of manufacturers rose. The wooden propellers of these old crafts are not only beautifully made, but have the elegance of works of sculpture.

One of the most successful, if not the most successful, manufacturers of fighter aircraft was the British and Colonial Aeroplane

Company, formed in 1910 by Bristol businessman Sir George White and later renamed the Bristol Aeroplane Company. Their first effort, the Boxkite, was a pusher biplane that can still be seen in the Bristol City Museum. White took the very sensible decision to set up flying schools, so that would-be purchasers could actually become familiar with the craft – and those who just came for lessons might be persuaded to buy. By the start of the war, the works were kept busy, particularly building the B.E. fighters, designed by the Royal Aircrafts establishment at Farnborough. The aircraft proved no match for the German fighters, and, faced with severe losses, the chief engineer Captain Frank Barnwell set about designing a new aircraft. The first version proved to be underpowered, but a new engine became available, the 190hp from Rolls Royce. Barnwell redesigned the whole plane to fit the new requirements, and the result was the F.2A –invariably simply known as the Bristol Fighter. It was a two-seater biplane, with the observer sat behind the pilot, provided with a seat that could be folded away for combat, when the observer stood to fire a Lewis machine gun. The first trials were disappointing and baffled the designer, because the plane had a ceiling of just 6,000ft. It was the test pilot who eventually located the problem: it was not the plane that was at fault, but the altimeter giving a false reading. Such were the problems facing designers in those days.

Bristol, like many other companies, began to employ women in the war years. The extra help was certainly needed, as following the first order of fifty fighter aircraft in the summer of 1916, their success in combat resulted in orders for a further 600. As in other industries, there were initial doubts about having women working alongside the men. They were strictly segregated, and the government helped to provide the funds for a separate canteen. It was soon found that, with suitable training, there were few jobs that the women could not manage. One type of work, however, was given almost entirely to the women. The fuselage of a plane was created by stretching material, usually linen, over the steel or wooden frame. Then to make it airtight and watertight, it had to be 'doped', treated with a lacquer made from cellulose acetate. The dope itself had originally come from

Switzerland, but at the start of the war, the two brothers Henri and Camille Dreyfus, who owned a factory in Basle, set up a new business in Derbyshire. Cellulose acetate is highly toxic, and many of the women suffered from headaches, nausea and fatigue. They were given milk to drink, a 'cure' of very dubious value. The ill-effects were, not surprisingly, similar to those in the munitions industry, where women were working with nitrocellulose to make guncotton.

The aircraft industry developed at a quite astonishing rate during the war years, in every respect. As technology advanced, so the way in which the planes were used changed as well. At first, they were seen as merely aids to observation of troop movements, and air-to-air fights consisted of little more than pilots taking pot shots at each other with pistols. Later, with the mounting of machine guns, the fighters became altogether more effective. The big advance came with the introduction of the forward-firing machine gun. Using synchronising gear, it was timed so that it could be fired through the propeller blades. The British version was made by Vickers, and it meant that the pilots no longer had to rely on their observers for firepower. They didn't need to manoeuvre to get into a position from where the other man could get a clear shot – now they simply pointed the plane at the enemy. Perhaps the most telling statistics that show how far technology had moved comes from the bombers. In 1907, the first single-engined British military aircraft had staggered into the sky for a flight, with just one man on board, which scarcely lasted half a minute. By 1918 a new generation of bombers was setting off on missions, armed with massive bombs. The Handley Page V/1500 was a four-engined biplane that could take off from England for raids over Berlin, and the biggest bombs available were now a massive 1,650lb. Ultimately, the aeroplane was to prove more effective than the airship, particularly after the introduction of the incendiary bullet. In the early days, a direct hit on a Zeppelin was likely to do little more than cause a small, repairable hole in just one of the gas bags. With the introduction of the new bullet, trailing its stream of burning phosphorus, the air ship would become a fireball of burning hydrogen.

It is doubtful if any technology had ever advanced so quickly before; and probably no such giant strides would be made again until the development of electronics in the computer age. But unlike other technological advances, it was not merely down to the brilliance of engineers and designers, but also due to the daring of the pioneers, prepared to take to the skies in untried and untested machines. Our next industry could scarcely be a greater contrast: from something brand new to one ages old; from up in the air to deep underground.

13

DEEP
UNDERGROUND

At the start of the war, metal mines, apart from the ironstone mines already discussed in chapter 6, were in a state of terminal decline. One of the last of the great copper mines, Devon Great Consols, had sold over £3 million worth of copper ore in the last decade of the nineteenth century, roughly £180 million at today's prices, but it went into liquidation in 1901 with the loss of over 350 jobs. The position in coal mining, however, was very different. At the start of the war, the industry was booming, but fragmented. There were 3,289 working collieries in Britain, producing 287 million tons of coal. Demand had never been higher. The move from country to town that was a major feature of the industrial changes of the nineteenth century, meant that families could no longer go out into the woods and fields to collect firewood, but relied on coal to heat their homes. The development of steam power for industry and transport created another new demand. The introduction of gas lighting called for yet more coal for manufacturing the raw material, and even the development of electric lighting did nothing to reduce the demand: the new power stations mostly depended on steam turbines, many of which still used coal as a fuel to produce the steam. There were signs of changes ahead with the rapid development of the internal combustion engine that would create demand for a new fuel, oil, but that still lay in the future. In the meantime, there was also a thriving export trade: about one-third of Britain's coal output was sent abroad.

War brought one immediate problem to the industry: the export market was soon badly affected by the war at sea, but there remained a more serious difficulty. Relations between masters and men in the coal industry were probably worse than in any other of Britain's workplaces. Partly it was due to the fragmented nature of the business: it was not easy for miners in South Wales, for example, to make common cause with those in Durham or Scotland. This meant that it had proved extremely difficult to create national unions, so that when industrial action hit one region, the shortfall in production could always be made up from other coalfields. It also made it easy for owners to target weaknesses among their local employees. Many miners lived in houses owned by the mine owners and could be, and often had been, evicted with their families when they went on strike. Add to that a long history of employing blackleg labour and it is easy to see why masters and men seemed to exist in a more or less constant state of mutual antagonism. It was never going to be easy to get the miners to agree to the deal worked out between Lloyd George and the trade union movement that banned strikes and go-slows in favour of compulsory arbitration and accepted dilution, bringing in outsiders to work in the different industries.

In spite of the loss of export markets, coal was still vital to the country's survival, and mining needed a huge number of workers. At the same time, there was also a demand for miners to carry out a specialist task for the army. Once the long line of trenches that formed the Western Front had been established, it was soon recognised that there was more than one way to attack the enemy lines. Tens of thousands of men went 'over the top', but very many also went burrowing underground to lay explosive charges beneath the German fortifications. This was a job for which the miners were uniquely well trained, so recruiting officers toured the mining districts, offering them a special pay rate of 6s per day. Miners were swept up by the waves of patriotism breaking across the country, just like almost everyone else, though the pay no doubt helped to feed their enthusiasm. Altogether some 40,000 miners signed up.[1]

The work of these military miners, the sappers, was as arduous as working in a coal mine, but with added dangers. Typically they would sink a shaft to a depth of some 20–30ft, and then begin tunnelling from the foot of the shaft, heading off towards the enemy lines. Tunnels did not have to be generously sized: it was only intended that they would be used once. A typical tunnel was 4ft wide by 3ft high. Because of the cramped conditions, only small gangs were used – usually four working at the face in relays, two more hauling away the spoil and another working the air pumps that were necessary to keep the air breathable. It was essential to work as quietly as possible and there was always the awareness that while the British were burrowing their way towards the Germans, they might always have the chance of meeting a German tunnel coming the other way.

Lt Geoffrey Boothby was in charge of a tunnelling squad: it was typical that the officer in charge, unlike the NCOs, would have had no experience whatsoever of the mining industry. He had in fact just started a medical degree when he left his studies to join the army. However, he and a small party set out to inspect an old tunnel, where someone had discovered a German telephone. This tunnel had been used by the Germans as a drain, pumping out water from their own workings, so that the inspection party had to slosh through water about 1ft deep. It was not a peaceful, secretive progress, and when they reached a point where the tunnel turned through a right-angle, someone started shooting at them. The rifleman had no need to expose himself to any return fire by the British: all he had to do was poke his gun round the corner and pull the trigger, with a fair chance in that confined space of hitting someone. Miraculously, none of the British party was injured as they retreated as much speed they could manage, splashing through the water and crouched beneath the low roof. They were back shortly afterwards, armed not with rifles but with explosives to close off the tunnel for good – hoping to trap the enemy before they trapped them. Boothby's luck deserted him a year later, when a bomb went off in another tunnel he was inspecting: his body was never recovered.[2]

It has been estimated that altogether around 8,000 miles of tunnels were dug during the war, and explosives laid often with devastating effect, but nowhere more so than in the Battle of Messines Ridge, northern France, in 1917. The Germans had occupied the high ground outside the village of Messines since the Western Front had first been established. Charging across no-man's-land was never going to dislodge them, but attack from underneath could succeed. The tunnelling had begun eighteen months before the start of the offensive, and a total of twenty-two tunnels were completed, in each of which massive charges of explosives were laid, totalling nearly 450 tons. The charges were to be set off on the morning of 7 June. The officer in charge of the operations, General Plummer, was heard to remark: 'Gentlemen, we may not make history tomorrow, but we shall certainly change the geography.' The German positions had been subjected to a relentless bombardment, and at ten minutes to three that day, the artillery barrage restarted, usually the overture to an attack over no-man's-land, and it sent the Germans scurrying to their defensive positions, right on top of the hidden explosives. Twenty minutes later the charges went off, with deafening explosions that were said to have been heard in Downing Street, where Lloyd George was waiting to hear the news of the assault, and great columns of earth were thrown into the sky reaching a height as high as the dome of St Paul's Cathedral. Altogether about 10,000 German soldiers were killed. Those who remained were deafened by the noise and had no time to recover from the shock before another example of Britain's new technology appeared over the horizon to completely demoralise the troops. The new improved Mk IV tanks lumbered over the battlefield, destroying the barbed wire defences, to be followed by the infantry. Thousands of prisoners were taken. History was made, and the geography was indeed altered. Today the scene at Messines Ridge is marked by a series of ornamental lakes, all that remain of the giant craters blown from the earth that summer morning in 1917.

Back in Britain the miners, like every other worker, were faced with the new restrictions laid down in the Munitions Act of 1915. It was widely welcomed by many employers, not just in the mining industry. An editorial in *Flight* magazine expressed the views of many of them – trade union action was described as 'the misuse of the power of slackers and inefficients, for the protection of their own laziness and short comings by cute officials who have to make and keep jobs for themselves'. Many mine owners took a similar view of their workers and shared the loathing of trade unionists. The official report of the Mines Department of November 1916 dealt with the problem of absenteeism in a rather more sympathetic manner. It began by putting the problem in its historic context: 'Owing to the arduous character of their labours miners do not work six full days in the week.' It estimated absenteeism as running between 10 and 11 per cent of official work time, though did point out that included in those figures was time taken off for 'accident or sickness'. According to the mine owners, there was no point in ever increasing pay as it only encouraged the miners to take even more time off to spend the extra money. They used the argument again, when discussing 1916 wage levels. The report was having none of it:

> This apprehension, however, has not been borne out by the event. Appeals to the patriotism of miners has counteracted this tendency and though there is still a regrettable amount of absenteeism, there is nevertheless a reduction amounting to almost 20 per cent in the amount of absenteeism which may be taken to be avoidable.

Though the government reports resolutely failed to back the more extreme charges of many mine owners that workers in the industry were lazy and overpaid, this did not stop the employers pushing for what they described as essential reforms that were needed for wartime conditions. These included cancelling the Eight Hours Act that limited underground shifts, something for which mining unions had fought for many years before it was finally passed by Parliament. They also pushed for reducing holiday time and increasing productivity targets. At no point in their representations to the government did they suggest putting any limits on extra profits that might be made by implementing these measures. Given the great gulf between the two sides, the mining unions did not sign the Treasury Agreements, and when a wage claim put in early in 1915 in South Wales was rejected, the men came out on strike, which was illegal under the new laws. The union was unable to give out strike pay without breaking the law, so the action was strictly unofficial. But as no one considered it sensible to try and send 200,000 essential workers to prison, the whole affair was settled by arbitration. Nevertheless, some sort of action was felt necessary, and seven of the strike leaders were sent to jail. The government, however, was not going to accept such a situation in the long term, and they took away the negotiating rights of both sides in the valleys and handed responsibility to a government-appointed coal controller. Although relations in South Wales had for a long time been worse than in any other region, the system soon spread to all of Britain's collieries. The country's mines were under government control.

Throughout the war, the government played an increasingly important part in controlling wages, but pay rises steadily fell behind the cost of living increases and the mining industry was hit as hard as any. The government's own survey of the situation, spelled out in a Ministry of Labour report of October 1917, put figures to go with the facts. Since the start of the war there had 'probably' been a rise of 35–40 per cent in pay, but during the same time the cost of essentials had risen by 80 per cent. In their own words, it was officially accepted that 'the great bulk of the working classes would appear to be in a much worse position than before the war'. Yet in spite of this, the notoriously militant mine unions mostly remained at work. There were, however, other aspects of the wartime legislation that they resisted fiercely, particularly dilution. In the mining industry there was never any notion of recruiting women to work underground, but the miners were equally opposed to any inexperienced men being brought in to share their work. To understand why they were so vehement in their opposition you have to understand something of the nature of the industry as it existed at the start of the war.

A certain amount of mechanisation had appeared in the industry by the start of the twentieth century. Blasting was an essential part of the process of extracting the coal, and the first stage involved drilling into the rock to make holes that would be filled with the explosive charge. This work that had once been done by hand was made far easier by the introduction of the pneumatic drill. There had been numerous attempts to design powered coal cutters, but they had failed due to the lack of a suitable power source. This was only really solved with the introduction of compressors powered by electricity. Even so, at the start of the twentieth century little more than 1 per cent of coal in British mines was cut by machinery. Even with automatic cutters, there was still a lot of work that was done by hand, and that included loading the coal into tubs to be taken to the bottom of the shaft, where they could be carried up to the surface in a cage, usually powered by a steam engine. This system too was starting to change, when W.C. Blackett invented an endless steel conveyor belt that was first installed in a Durham colliery, followed three years later by George Sutcliffe's version introduced into Yorkshire. Even where mechanisation was brought in, the life of the miner was little easier than it had been before. George Orwell wrote his impression of a visit to a mine and, although written after the war, it would be applicable to the most modern pits during the war years:

> The first impression of all, overmastering everything else for a while, is the frightful, deafening din from the conveyor belt which carries the coal away. You cannot see very far because the fog of coal dust throws back the beam of your lamp, but you can see on either side of you the line of half-naked, kneeling men, one to every four or five yards, driving their shovels under the fallen coal and flinging it swiftly over their left shoulders. They are feeding it onto the conveyor belt, a moving rubber belt a couple of feet wide which runs a yard or two behind them. Down this belt a glittering river of coal races constantly … It is a dreadful job that they do, an almost superhuman job by the standards of an ordinary person. For they are not only shifting monstrous quantities of coal, they are also doing it in a position that doubles or trebles the work. They have got to remain kneeling all the while – they could hardly rise from their knees without hitting the ceiling – and you can

easily see by trying it what a tremendous effort this means. Shovelling is comparatively easy when you are standing up, because you can use your knee and thigh to drive the shovel along: kneeling down, the whole of the strain is thrown upon your arm and belly muscles. And the other conditions do not exactly make things easier. There is the heat – it varies, but in some mines it is suffocating – and the coal dust that stuffs up your throat and nostrils and collects along your eyelids, and the unending rattle of the conveyor belt, which in that confined space is rather like the rattle of a machine gun.[3]

In 1914 not all pits were even this sophisticated, and working by hand in a narrow seam was even worse than Orwell's description of the men feeding the conveyor. At times, a man was reduced to lying on his side, with the top of the coal face just inches above his head, hacking away at the seam with a pickaxe. Pit ponies were used in many mines to move the coal from face to surface, but in some the work was still done by men and boys, pushing the loaded tubs by hand.

The world of the miner was unique. It was not simply a matter of the immensely hard physical labour: it was also about having to work in conditions that most people could scarcely imagine. At the start of a shift, the men would go down in the cage but then often have a long trudge to the face, sometimes down passageways so low that their bodies were bent almost double. There would be no light apart from the lights they brought with them, the safety lamps that offered a dim light at best. Once they reached the face they would stay there all day: the only food and drink they would have would be what they brought with them, and they would take their breaks in the gloom of the pit. Sanitary arrangements were simply non-existent. At the end of the day, there was the same trudge back to the cage to be returned to the surface. Pithead baths were a rarity, so the men went home in their filth, often to houses where the bath was a galvanised tub in the kitchen, filled with water heated on a stove. This was not a way of life that would readily appeal to anyone not brought up in the mining community – which was why during the Second World War, when there was a serious manpower shortage, the government had to bring in conscripts, the famous Bevin Boys. It was not just the working conditions that made mining different from other industries: there were also the dangers.

The introduction of the safety lamp in the early nineteenth century was supposed to put an end to the tragedies caused by explosions. What was not realised was that although the lamp removed the danger of igniting methane, then known as fire damp, it did nothing to prevent explosions from an unrecognised killer – coal dust. In 1913, 462 miners were killed by explosions and 131 were injured. These were dramatic events, which were actually made worse by the introduction of labour-saving devices: the new drills and cutters created far more dust than older devices. And the fog of dust so vividly described by Orwell was highly volatile – one spark was all that was needed to cause an explosion.

Explosions are only a part of the story. In that same year, the deaths from accidents in mines were 1,753, while 177,189 were injured.[4] Official statistics showed that more men were killed by what was described as 'falling ground' than by explosions. In other words, men were buried under collapsing roofs. Often this happened simply because the pressure to send a certain number of tubs filled with coal to the surface each day was so great that men were reluctant to take time away from that job to fit in extra supports. The figures had nothing to say about the many more who died from lung disease. That was accepted with a certain grim fatalism. I remember visiting a colliery and mentioning to a miner that I'd been surprised to find that I was still blowing coal dust out of my nose many days after my last visit. 'Ay', replied the miner, 'but it's what you don't blow out that'll kill you.'

The government passed an act in 1911 that established an inspectorate in an attempt to solve the problem of mine accidents, but at the start of the war there were only seventy-four mine inspectors, who seldom had time to spend more than a few hours at each site actually looking at conditions underground. Even when pits were inspected and faults pointed out, there was no guarantee that any action would be quickly taken: managers knew that a year could go by before anyone arrived to check up if recommendations had been carried out. The explosion at Senghenydd Colliery in October 1913 was almost certainly caused by a spark from bare wires used in the electric signalling system, a fault that had already been pointed out. As a result 439 men died.

In practice, the miners relied heavily on each other to try and maintain safety standards and, when accidents did occur, to carry out essential rescue work. They had little faith in the inspectorate, and none in the justice system that dealt with responsibility for the tragedies. The manager at Senghenydd was found guilty on six charges of negligence, three of which were considered likely to have had a direct effect on the accident. He was fined £24. The local newspaper bitterly reported that now they knew what value was placed on a miner's life: 1s 1¼d each.

The essentials of the industry had changed little over the centuries. Other industries could locate their factories in appropriate towns: in the mining industry the pits came first and the towns grew up around the spots where they were sunk. As a result, in a mining village virtually everyone's life was closely tied to the fortunes of the pit. It made for a very closed community, where people relied on each other and men depended for their lives on the skill and experience of those who worked alongside them. In these circumstances, there was very little chance of inexperienced strangers being made welcome, nor if they did arrive could they expect to take on any job that might put others in danger. This was an industry where dilution was not a realistic option. Nor was it an industry that was going to give up rights and privileges for which they had fought long and hard. The replacement of the former owners by a government-appointed controller was not going to change old attitudes.

Discontent in the mining areas grew steadily, particularly in south Wales, where an arbitration agreement had been agreed in 1910 but it expired in March 1915. In 1916 the Welsh put in for a wage rise, threatening strike action. Lloyd George went in person to Cardiff to meet the miners' leaders in the hope of reaching an easy settlement. The dispute was settled but wage demands were made again in 1917 and the whole matter was referred to the War Cabinet, who were given an official report on the situation:

> The Coal Committee stated that the men were out of hand, and the leaders were not leading but being pushed ... the men based their claim on the fact that the cost of living had risen during the war by 83 per cent. They also alleged that 50 per cent of the miners had to pay for tools, the cost of which had gone up during the war.[5]

The cabinet was reluctant to give a rise on the basis of rising costs on the grounds that it would encourage other industrial workers, faced with the same situation, to put in their own demands. On the other hand, they could not afford the loss of coal production. The coal controller was authorised to negotiate, with a limit set at 'a maximum of 1s 8d per day and 10d per day for boys'. He did rather better than that, reaching agreement at 1s 6d and 9d for the two rates. The emergency was averted.

Apart from the removal of wage rate settlements from private hands to the government, very little changed in the coal industry during the war years. The supply of coal was maintained and men continued to work much as they had in the nineteenth century, under often atrocious conditions, without complaining. In spite of suspicions that owners were making large profits while wages were kept low, there was very little in the way of industrial action. The miners did their part in the coalfields of Britain and beneath the fields of Flanders.

14

TEXTILES

The textile industry lay at the very heart of the Industrial Revolution that by the end of the eighteenth century had transformed British society. It had begun with a huge demand for cotton cloth, light and colourful in comparison with the rather drab woollens of earlier times. By the 1830s it was claimed that the cotton industry had grown to such an extent 'that the yarn spun in this country would, in a single thread, pass round the globe's circumference 203,775 times'.[1] By that time, virtually all the processes involved in turning a raw material into finished cloth had been moved from the home to the factory, thanks to British inventiveness. What had begun with cotton soon spread to the older woollen industry. At first the mills had all been powered by water, but in the nineteenth century more and more were powered by steam engines, a technology also pioneered in Britain, and by the time of the First World War, some factories were enormous and the engines that powered them equally gargantuan. These monsters were still being installed in the early twentieth century.

It is still possible to see one of these great engines steamed in its original setting at Trencherfield Mill, a former cotton-spinning mill beside the Leeds & Liverpool Canal in Wigan. This is a four-cylinder triple expansion engine, which simply means that it is worked by high-pressure steam, which is still under considerable pressure when it leaves the first cylinder, so the exhaust steam can be fed into a second, intermediate cylinder to do more work, and from that can go to the pair of low-pressure cylinders. Built in 1907, it needed to be huge, as it has to drive all the machinery of a mill built with four storeys and a basement. This was done through an immense flywheel, 26ft in diameter, which has fifty-four grooves round the perimeter. Each of these grooves holds a rope that is used to turn shafts through a pulley system. The shafts turn on every floor of the building throughout the mill, and from these shafts leather belts take the power down to the individual machines. That is a lot of work for one engine, but it does generate an impressive 2,500hp.

The steam engine is not an efficient machine, in the sense that the ratio of the amount of power it produces to the amount of energy that has to be supplied in terms of burning fuel to create the steam – the thermal efficiency – is very low. This was not a great problem in the north of England where coal was readily available. It was to cause difficulties in the traditional woollen cloth-making area of the west of England, which had been built up on the basis of water power. The industry there was in decline. Stroud, the town at the heart of the Gloucestershire woollen industry, could once boast 100 mills within 10 miles of the town centre. Many had closed by the start of the twentieth century and it is ironic that the area was to play a comparatively small part in the war effort, for Stroud had once been famous for its scarlet cloth: for generations it had supplied the material for the uniforms of the British Army, but that was before the advent of the powerful, accurate rifle. Wearing a scarlet tunic in battle was rather like waving a flag, with the message 'Shoot me'. The red tunics were only retained for ceremonial occasions for some regiments, mostly the Guards.

There was another problem with the steam engine. The whole mighty engine had to be run before any machinery at all could be made to work. By the beginning of the twentieth century, more and more mills were looking to electricity as a source of power, but because the national network did not exist, most had to generate their own supplies. For some, which had been sited close to sources of water in earlier times, it was possible to use water turbines to turn the generators. Others relied on steam engines to turn the generators, though these were very puny affairs compared with the mighty mill engines. Later, diesel engines could be used. At the former Longford's woollen mill in Gloucestershire, the powerhouse still has all three in place: water turbines, steam and diesel engines. Once electric power was in place, the old system of overhead line shafting and constantly turning leather belts could be replaced by machines, each of which had its individual motor. When mains electricity arrived, the electrically powered mill became an obvious choice for manufacturers. In the years up to and including the First World War, this process of change was still under way, as more and more mills converted to electricity.

There had been other changes in the industry in the years following the first burst of vital activity. Samuel Crompton had invented his mule for spinning fibres at the end of the eighteenth century, and it had been greatly improved in the nineteenth, but suffered from one disadvantage. The biggest mules had up to 1,000 spindles, each one of which was spinning yarn, which was wound onto bobbins – but whenever the bobbins were full, the whole machine had to be stopped, the full bobbins 'doffed', that is removed, and replaced by new, empty bobbins, to which threads had to be attached ready to restart the spinning process. A different system, the ring frame, was introduced from America later in the nineteenth century, which could be run continuously.

Innovation was continuing throughout all the different processes, but never as dramatically as in the early years of industrial processing. Basically, for both cotton and woollen mills, the processes involved were similar. Bales of raw material had to be broken open, and the fibres of wool or cotton untangled and aligned in a process that could be either 'carding' or 'combing'. The material could then be spun, an operation that involved stretching out the fibres and twisting them together. The yarn was now ready to be placed on the loom for weaving into cloth. The first part of the process involved warping, winding the yarn in a specified order round a roller that was placed at the back of the loom, and the threads then passed through loops in wires, so that alternate threads could be raised and lowered. The weft threads were placed in a shuttle, which was thrown backwards and forwards between the warp threads, to create an interlocking weave. For complex patterns, warping involved arranging many different coloured threads in the right order, and drop shuttle looms allowed weft threads of different colours to be placed in the shuttles, which then had to be thrown in the correct sequence. It was a complex business and all of this description is, of course, a considerable over-simplification of a number of complex processes. But in a factory full of powered machinery, there was one thing all the machines had in common: they made a tremendous racket.

It is difficult for those who have never visited a working mill to realise just what it is like. To take just one part of the process, weaving: you have to envisage overhead line shafting, with hundreds of creaking, iron pulleys turning relentlessly all day long. Down below would be row upon row of power looms, in each one of which a shuttle is being thrown from one side to the other to the accompaniment of a bang at the end of each throw. It is impossible to have a normal conversation: the only way to make yourself heard is to put your mouth next to the other person's ear and shout. I remember being in such a mill, when the supervisor suddenly yelled: 'I've got to go – my phone's ringing.' For a moment I was baffled, until he pointed to a flashing light over the office door. Most mill workers soon learned to lip-read. To anyone like myself, brought up in the West Riding of Yorkshire, the heart of the woollen industry, it was a common experience to sit next to someone on the top of a double-decker bus who was having a conversation with a friend down below at the bus stop, with neither of them making an audible sound. Deafness was a real problem for many workers in later life.

The noise was not the only hazard faced by mill workers. In the early years of the twentieth century, safety precautions were few. Dust from cotton or wool fibres flew everywhere and respiratory diseases were common. It was not the only things that flew around the mill. According to one worker in a Gloucestershire mill, it was quite common for shuttles to depart from the loom like missiles, and 'many finished up going to hospital'.[2] Accidents could happen almost anywhere, even in what must have seemed comparatively safe operations. As part of the finishing process for woollens, the cloth had to be passed through a milling machine, which shrank it and brought the fibres together. It was fed through rollers as a continuous loop, so first the ends had to be sewn together using a heavy industrial sewing machine. On one occasion, a worker was looking after two of these machines, and managed to put the needle right through his finger. A mechanic had to be brought to free the needle from the machine, and in the meantime a lad was sent to fetch a cup of tea for the victim. The tea arrived, the lad took one look at the impaled finger and passed out: he was given the tea. Eventually the unfortunate sewer went to the local hospital, where the needle was removed. He asked to be given the needle – 'it was company property'.

Even in areas that were free from the racket of machinery they were not always pleasant places to work. Dye houses were an essential part of most mills, though there were also independent dye works. In the case of woollens, dyeing could take place at the end of weaving, or at the very beginning of the processes using the natural wool. In the latter case, the colour penetrated every fibre, hence a 'dyed in the wool' villain was one whose villainy ran right through his being. A description of a dye house of 100 years ago claimed it was like 'a scene from Dante's Inferno'. Men worked stripped to the waist, 'dressed only in loin cloths', poling the cloth in vast, steaming vats.

Textiles were hugely important to the British economy, and that importance grew steadily throughout the nineteenth century. In Yorkshire alone, there were over 600 mills in the woollen and worsted branches, employing some 40,000 workers in 1835. By the end of the century, there were over 1,500 mills and the workforce had expanded to 200,000.[3] A similar story could be told of the Lancashire cotton industry. Oldham was at the heart of their spinning industry: at the start of the war over one-quarter of the cotton spun in the whole country was spun in this one town. There were 360 mills, working night and day and employing some 40,000 people. Keeping production going was clearly important, but the industry did not face the same problem that faced others. Dilution was not an issue: women already made up the vast majority of the workforce. There is a popular image of the mill girls, seen pouring out of the factory gates, clogs on their feet and shawls thrown across their shoulders. This is not just a figment of romantic imagination. What the image does not show is the hard work that these girls and women had to do.

Working days were long and getting to work on time was not something you did just to keep the boss happy. Anyone arriving late could find the door shut in their face and could lose that day's wages. One Gloucestershire mill worker described having got up in the morning to find a heavy snowfall had covered the ground overnight. She had a long trudge through deep drifts, but eventually struggled in a few minutes late. She lost half a day's pay. She explained the circumstances and was simply told she should have allowed for the snow and started out earlier. It is no wonder that in many mill towns there were 'knockers-up' – men with long sticks that they would use to rap on bedroom windows to tell the sleepers it was time to rise.

The work itself could be demanding. The spinning mule consisted of a fixed frame, fitted with rollers that drew out the yarn, which then passed to hundreds of spindles mounted on a wheeled carriage. The carriage constantly moved backwards and forwards. On its outer journey from the main frame, the fibres were stretched even further and twisted by the revolving spindles. There was then a slight pause, before the carriage returned, and the spun fibre was wound onto bobbins. The girl in charge would walk backwards and forwards as the carriage moved, repairing broken threads – and in the course of a day she would have covered many miles to the accompaniment of the usual deafening racket. It was never an easy life.

The start of the war brought a new challenge to the woollen industry. Men were joining up in their tens and thousands and they all had to be kitted out. An idea of just how great that challenge was can be gauged from just one uniform distribution centre. The tram sheds at Swinegate in Leeds had been taken over and turned into the Northern Area Clothing Depot. From there they sent out 53 million shirts, 29 million tunics, 89 million pairs of socks and 10 million great coats – 75,000 different items of clothing had to be inspected every day. Providing uniforms in such quantities was vital. At the end of 1916, in order to ensure that supplies of raw material were always available in the right quantity and at a reasonable price, the government took control of all wool purchases.

A new technology had been developed during the nineteenth century that made the production of woollen uniform cloth easier and considerably more economical than it would have been had everything had to be made from the pure wool of fleeces straight from the sheep. This new technique used rags as the raw material – loosely woven rags produced 'shoddy' and hard rags produced 'mungo'. These were collected by the rag and bone man, who toured the streets with his traditional cry of 'rags, bottles and bones' – all materials that could be reused in various ways – bottles recycled, bones made into glue. The Yorkshire shoddy works were mostly concentrated in an area round Dewsbury: they were not savoury places in which to work. The first part of the process was carbonising. There were two methods used. Wet carbonising involved soaking the rags in pits full of acid. Dry carbonising was used for rags that had a mixture of cotton and wool. Acid was heated to produce gas, which was then fed through cages containing the rags. In this process the cotton content was destroyed. The rags were then shredded and ground in 'devils'. The manufacture of shoddy involved the workers spending their days in an atmosphere heavy with fumes and fine fibre particles, and the works themselves were notorious for their high fire risk. It was not a healthy occupation, but was one that was important to the war effort. Shoddy and mungo, mixed with wool, was the raw material from which cloth for the army uniforms and greatcoats were made.

The actual making of the garments from cloth was also itself a major industry. A popular song from the early years of the war suggested that it was all down to individuals working at home, as if the Industrial Revolution had never happened; 'Sister Susie's Sewing Shirts for Soldiers':

Sister Susie's sewing in the kitchen on a Singer
There's miles and miles of flannel on the floor and up the stairs,
And father says it's rotten getting mixed up with the cotton
And sitting on the needles that she leaves upon the chairs.

In reality, the provision of clothing for the troops had little to do with individuals working at home with patriotic fervour. The actual job of making the shirts and the uniforms from the cloth provided by the textile mills was down to the workers of what was then a comparatively new industry, that of the clothiers, manufacturers of ready-made clothing. It relied on the use of industrial sewing machines, developed out of the domestic machines of the type patented by Isaac Singer in America in 1851. Jobs that had been done by seamstresses, usually working for pittances in sweatshops, now went to workshops and factories. Leeds was the centre of activity and, by the start of the war, had literally hundreds of premises, large and small, and more were started up during the war to meet the growing demand. Some, such as Arthur & Co., were employing over 1,500 workers, of whom 900 were women. Others such as Montague Burton, a Lithuanian émigré who had established his first business in Chesterfield with a loan of £100 when he was just 18 years old, had moved to Leeds and prospered during the war years. Burton's were to grow to such an extent that by the time of the Second World War, they had become so big that they manufactured one-quarter of all the British uniforms made between 1939 and 1945.[4]

The Yorkshire woollen industry thrived during the war years, but the situation was completely different in the other great textile industry – cotton. Where wool manufacturers had relied largely on supplying a home market and was now facing increased demand, the cotton industry exported much of its product. Before the war, Britain had sent 33 million pounds of yarn per year to Germany and 6 million pounds to Turkey. Those markets were instantly lost, and by 1915, the export trade had dropped by 20 per cent. This was not the only blow to fall on the industry. It relied on imports of raw material, largely from America and to a lesser extent from India, to keep the mills busy, and as the war against merchant ships grew in ferocity so supplies began to dry up. To some extent the effects on employment were not as bad as they might have been, as so many men had volunteered for active service – 5,000 had left from Oldham alone. But it was disastrous for the tens of thousands of women who worked in the industry. Demand too began to change – now mainly for the coarser yarns, which meant altering some of the existing machinery. But the good news as far as the manufacturers were concerned was that there was still a high demand for cotton at home, and shortages drove up prices: profits by the end of 1916 had risen by an average of 11 per cent. It was not such good news for the workforce. Many mills went on short time and wages fell, while even those in work felt they were falling behind in earning power as costs rose.

At the beginning of 1917, the carders who worked on the first stage in the production process put in for a 10 per cent pay rise: 'The employers, taking into account the vastly increased cost of everything and the undesirableness of advancing the price of cotton cloth to prohibitive heights, firmly opposed any concession.'[5] The demand was referred to the government arbitrator, who awarded a 5 per cent rise. 'The operatives were highly disappointed with this decision, urging that it was in flat defiance of the facts and roundly declaring that it had for ever obliterated any faith they might have had at any time in the merits of compulsory arbitration.' The situation deteriorated still further through the first part of the year, and the operatives were still complaining about the rise of profits and the fall in their own living standards: 'Chief among the causes of working class anger was the fact that, in spite of much brave talk, little had been done to stamp out profiteering.'[6]

The greatest problem facing the industry was getting in supplies of raw cotton. The situation worsened in 1917 when America entered the war. They had plenty of cotton to send to Britain, but there was a severe shortage of ships to send it in. Quite apart from the damage done to British merchant shipping, available ships were now being used to bring American troops and supplies to Europe. Something had to be done to remedy an increasingly desperate situation and employers and trade unionists got together to work out a rota, where the work could be shared out. It was not entirely satisfactory and many of the women and girls who had worked in the mills left to find other work, largely in munitions. There was a demand for cotton for the forces fighting the campaigns in the Near East, but it did little to make up for the loss of other markets. It was at least good news for the industry in India, the country that had first introduced colourful cotton cloth to Britain, creating the demand. Once the British started importing raw cotton, instead of finished products, India suffered from competition from Lancashire, thanks largely to tariffs imposed by the British government. Now it was India's turn to make the most of a new opportunity. They were in a much better position to help with the needs of the army in the east, and were able to pick up many of the markets once dominated by Lancashire. The industry boomed. More mills were built in India, more workers employed and cloth production rose from 1,164 million yards in 1914 to 1,614 million in 1917.[7]

Other textile industries also had a part to play in the war effort. Dundee became known as 'Juteopolis'. At the start of the war there were some sixty mills in the city employing around 50,000 workers. Now they acquired a special importance, for jute was the fibre used to manufacture sandbags. Probably no one ever worked out just how many sandbags were used for protection in the trenches of the Western Front, but it could well have run into millions and the vast majority relied on covers produced by the mills of Dundee.

The linen industry had been in decline for some time. It was traditionally associated with producing tablecloths and napkins, but now it had a new use. It was the first choice as the material for covering the fuselages of Britain's warplanes. No matter which aspect of the textile industry you look at, it seems that it had a vital role to play in the war effort. One other industry, traditionally associated with peace not war, was to prove equally important. Farming has traditionally been used to slow change rather than sudden convulsions of innovation, but it too had to adapt to the changing demands of war.

15

DOWN ON THE FARM

'The food question ultimately decided the issue of the War', according to Lloyd George.[1] This seems a remarkable statement and no one would have thought such an idea anything other than totally absurd when the war started. People did, however, think that during the short time that the war was expected to last there might be shortages, so there was an early period of panic buying. That soon settled down, and things appeared to be more or less returning to normal. It was only as the war dragged on and shipping losses mounted that food shortage started to become a major problem. For a time it did seem to be a real possibility that the country might not be beaten on the battlefield but in the kitchen, as the British went hungry. The problem was at least partly due to the way in which the industry had developed over the previous decades.

Farming changed throughout nineteenth-century Britain, perhaps not as spectacularly as other industries had done, and in agriculture those changes were not all down to increased mechanisation. New crops were brought in and improved fertilisers helped to increase yields. Food supplies had to be increased to meet the demands of a growing population: the numbers for England and Wales had been just 10 million in 1811, but at the start of the war they had risen to 37 million. There was, however, an important difference from earlier times: the extra food that was needed no longer had to be provided only from British farms. The repeal of the Corn Laws in 1846 removed the high tariffs imposed on imported grain, opening up the local market to the cheap wheat grown on the vast prairies of North America. At the same time, there was a growing demand at home for other produce, such as meat. Developments in refrigeration meant that meat could be brought in from abroad: by the beginning of the twentieth century, New Zealand was shipping 4 million sheep and lamb carcasses to Britain. There were, however, some changes that helped the local farmers.

The spread of the railways made it possible to provide fresh milk for towns on a daily basis, so more and more farmers began to turn former arable land into pasture for dairy herds. Many also found it more profitable to use fields that had once grown grain to turn them over to vegetables. The change accelerated at the end of the nineteenth century, particularly after a disastrous year of almost continuous rain in 1879, which ruined the grain crops. More and more imported wheat poured in to make up the loss, and the British grain farmer never really recovered his share of the market. This was the situation at the start of the war, which instantly reversed the trend. Inevitably the flood of imported grain began to ebb. In the early part of the century, 75 per cent of Britain's wheat, 50 per cent of meat and 40 per cent of butter was imported.[2] Farming no longer seemed quite as vital as it once had done, and the share of the entire gross domestic product, which had been around 20 per cent in the 1850s had fallen to just 7 per cent in 1914. The acreage being farmed also dropped substantially, particularly in the areas that had previously been used for wheat, but the public was not concerned: they were getting cheap food and that was what mattered to them, not where it came from.

A Royal Commission was set up in 1903 to investigate the problem, and decided cautiously that there might be a case for the government to interfere, but it probably wasn't necessary: 'even during a maritime war there will be no material diminution in their [wheat imports] volume'. As late as 1914, Lord Lucas of the Board of Trade noted that there was plenty of grain in store and 'no occasion whatever for public alarm'. These confident predictions were to prove disastrously wrong.

Farming was not exempt from the rush of young men leaving the industry to join the forces, and as it was still comparatively unmechanised the loss of manpower created immediate problems. The steam traction engine had been introduced in the nineteenth century, but on farms its use was largely limited to powering threshing machines at harvest time. It was not much use in cultivation, simply because of the weight bearing down on its iron wheels meaning it did too much damage to the soil. Special ploughing engines had been introduced. These worked in pairs, positioned at either side of the field. Each had a drum beneath the engine, which could wind and unwind a cable stretched between them. A plough was attached to the wire, which could be pulled across the field from engine to engine. At the end of each furrow, the ploughshares were reversed, the two engines moved forward, and the plough returned in the opposite direction. It was an expensive operation, requiring a specialist three-man team, one on each engine and a third to sit on and steer the plough. Only wealthy farms with large acreages used the system. Everyone else did as they had for centuries – ploughed with a team of horses. The horse was also used for all forms of transport on the farm. Even devices such as mechanical reapers, introduced from America, were horse drawn.

At the start of the war, the tractor powered by an internal combustion engine was still a novelty. In 1896 Richard Hornsby had built the first British tractor to be powered by an oil engine, and later changed it by adding caterpillar tracks, as described in chapter 10. It did not come into general use on farms. It was soon clear to the government that if Britain was to be fed, farms would need extra labour in the short term, and help towards mechanisation in the long term. In the summer of 1915, enlisted former farm workers were given two weeks special leave to help with the harvest. The following year the Food Production Department was created as part of the Ministry of Agriculture. It had the power to control all labour on the farm and to send in extra help when required. It was not universally welcomed. After the war, the then president of the Board of Agriculture, R.E. Prother, described it as 'blackleg labour on a massive scale'.[3]

By 1917, soldiers were being sent out to help on farms that could prove they were short-handed. The authorities asked for volunteers who had experience of ploughing and farm work. There was an initial rush of over 12,000 soldiers, many of whom proved to have had little or no experience of useful work such as ploughing, but no doubt thought life on the farm had to be better than staying in the trenches. In the event, several thousand were put on to farm work. It was good news for the farmer. He only had to pay the agreed minimum wage to the War Office, which generally meant that the soldiers came cheaper than the regular farm hands. Just as there was no shortage of volunteers for farm work, so there was no lack of farmers coming forward claiming they hadn't enough hands to do the work. One can see why this was called a blackleg scheme.

There was a mixed reaction to the use of soldiers. The Agricultural Wages Board reporting on the scheme at the end of the war noted that some farmers 'believe that the men sent them are those who are no use as soldiers or in any other capacity'. A farmer called Hancock, however, reported very favourably on his volunteer: 'He has already ploughed up to 10 acres of old turf besides cutting about 40 acres with the self-binder. If all men were as practical and willing, the farmers would have little occasion to grumble.'

The soldiers were not the only source of cheap labour. Prisoners of war were also drafted in for farm work. They had to work for a pittance – being paid only 1d or 1½d per hour – but the farmers had to pay just as much to the War Office for prisoners of war as they paid for British soldiers. They were cheap, but unfortunately they were not efficient. It was not their fault. They were being asked to do hard, manual labour on prison rations, which decreed that the midday meal would consist of 4oz of biscuits and 1oz of cheese, and this was supposed to see them through a twelve-hour working day. The farmers were not allowed to give them food, nor were they allowed to use their meagre wages to buy any. One set of Whitehall bureaucrats wanted to see prisoners working on farms; another set made regulations that ensured they wouldn't be up to the job. It made no sense, except to those who simply objected on principle to seeing Germans fed as well as the British they were being told to work alongside.

By 1917 the food shortage was becoming desperate, so the government came up with a new scheme: they would recruit women. They founded the Women's Land Army (WLA). Recruitment posters appeared everywhere addressed to 'The Women of the Nation' with suitable slogans, such as 'God speed the plough and the woman who drives it'. As soon as the scheme was announced, around 45,000 women volunteered. Selection centres were set up around the country, one of which opened at Edgbaston, Birmingham on 4 October 1917.[4] It was selecting workers for the whole of the Midlands. The women were split into three groups: those who had considerable experience, those who had worked on the land for at least six months and those who had done three months' work. They were then divided up again according to the jobs they proved capable of doing in a series of tests. The top category was those who could prove themselves able to harness and handle teams of horses for all the jobs around the farm, from ploughing to driving carts. This group also included the very small number who were able to plough with a tractor. The second group were described, rather inelegantly, as cowmen, who had to be able to milk by hand and by machine. The third category was the labourers, who did all the unpleasant jobs such as pulling root vegetables and hoeing. Other women could volunteer for forestry work. Out of the 45,000 who came forward, only 5,000 were accepted at first.

As the food situation worsened, the demand for labour increased. Early in 1918, the Food Production Department sent out a letter to all the regional offices to tell them that they now needed to 'raise 30,000 additional women this year, and to use a large percentage of them as unskilled labour'.[5] They were also urged 'to use to the utmost the 250,000 village women who are known to be available for work on the land'. They were to be taken on as forewomen. Where the ordinary WLA women were taken on at 18s per week, later rising to £1, the forewomen were to get 25s, but had to sign on for a minimum of six months and be prepared to go anywhere in the country. Some of the forewomen would be put in charge of a gang working for a single farmer, but others would be in charge of a gang that would work for several farmers in a district. The latter would be formed into a new 'Corps of Village Forewomen':

> It is essential that women of the right type should be recruited at once. They should be women who have knowledge of village life and country conditions, and should have experience of field work. They should be women who can lead others.
>
> In many parts of the country, suitable women will be found in the villages; in others they will be women who have worked with gangs since the War and who will have sufficient knowledge for the work.

Like other WLA women, they would be provided with uniforms, but could also buy extras at special prices, ranging from a pair of boots at 25s to 2s for a sou'wester.

It all sounded sensible and well organised, but there were inevitable difficulties in introducing such radical changes into the often deeply conservative farming community. The Pathé team filmed the WLA, showing girls living in a camp, being woken by a bugler and cooking in the open, rather as if they were all back in the Girl Guides, then going off to work alongside the men in cheerful harmony. The official report on the first eighteen months of the scheme suggested that the reality was slightly different, and made no attempt to hide the problem:

> The farmers generally were still sceptical as to the value of women labour and their womankind had often no place and certainly no welcome for the newcomer. The Land Army was a new idea, not only to the farmers but also to the women themselves. Both the need for such a body and the truth of the food position had to be brought home to the public.[6]

The Food Production Department had a team of organising secretaries who also acted as inspectors, and one of these, who remains anonymous, wrote up her own extensive notes on the women and the work. She went to see a forestry group working high in the Welsh hills, and admitted she had to stop several times along the way to get her breath back as she climbed the steep, stony path to where they were hard at work. They were working in pairs, one with a pickaxe, making holes; the other placing in the saplings and firming the earth round them: 'It is difficult to recognise in these bonnie girls with fresh complexions, some of the thin pasty faced recruits.'[7] There was also a scheme in place for other 'pasty faced recruits', though that was not how they were described in the official literature. They were girls from the munitions factories who had been 'overworked' and were sent to take jobs in the countryside to recover. If, after three weeks, they showed no great improvement, they were sent home and found different jobs. For many, however, the country life did bring real benefits. But not everyone was having such a satisfactory working life. The anonymous organising secretary's diary entry for 19 October 1917 told a very different story, and is worth quoting at length:

Yesterday I received a pitiful letter from Nellie Owen. She says she can't stick it any longer, the bailiff had told her he has no further work for her after the end of next week, and she wants to return home then and leave the Land Army. I have learned not to take such letters too seriously, but as I review her history and the pluck she has shown, I feel this case is different. She was one of our very first recruits, had previously been a milliner, and comes from a good respectable home in the busy part of a town. During her month's training she was slower than the other girls, but very conscientious and reliable and she improved steadily. Her first post was on a small hill farm where no land girl had previously been seen, and like all pioneers she had a good deal of prejudice to overcome. From there she and another L.A.A.S. was sent across the border to another County for harvest work. The older woman has now left and she is there alone. I rang up the Organising Secretary of the neighbouring County and she gave me a free hand to do whatever I thought best.

To-day I went to see Nellie. It was an 8 mile cycle ride from the nearest railway station and seemed to be several miles from any village shop or post office. After enquiries at the farm and her lodgings, I was directed to a potato field at some distance where I found her working with the men. She told me 'It's not the work (I like the work) but I have tried my best and feel I can't stick it any longer. My people said when I joined that I should never be able to stand it, and that has made me determined not to give in but now I feel I must give in and nothing will induce me to stay on after Saturday week. The bailiff says women are no good and the people here taunt me that I am taking a man's place and driving him to the Army. My landlady (formerly a housemaid at the Hall) disapproves of and looks down upon land girls and lets me know it. I am not allowed into the house without taking off my boots. No I can't stand it any longer.'

I looked round and felt that I too should have broken my heart had I been in her place – no encouragement and no friends. As it happens we are short of workers for a potato gang at B- next week, so I suggested to her that if I could get the farmer to release her to-morrow instead of the following Saturday, that she should work her last week in the Land Army with the other girls at B-. She agreed 'but only for a week'. I had not much difficulty with the bailiff, a bombastic man who was very anxious to impress me with his view that women would never be any good for land work. He had no complaints to make about this particular girl, but – Oh yes, if I wanted her to-morrow I could have her, it made no difference to him. My heart went out in sympathy to the plucky little girl who had stood two months of this sort of thing.

Prejudice against the female workers was sadly widespread and extended to disapproval of their unladylike working clothes, which included such shocking apparel as breeches, and their behaviour when off duty. The land girls worked hard and no doubt liked to have a good time when they had the rare opportunity for a bit of leisure, but it brought an official reprimand:

In some places there have been unfortunate occurrences:– National Service girls, without doing anything flagrantly wrong, have yet by their manners and behaviour produced an unfortunate impression. This is especially noticeable in County Towns – the uniform is discredited and the Government girls get a bad reputation. It has been suggested that wherever possible, Welfare Workers should encourage the formation of Committees among the girls themselves, and get them to inculcate the idea that the up-holding of the dignity of the uniform and of girl-hood is essential to carrying out the actual work.[8]

It clearly would never do to upset the good ladies of the county town!

The WLA did a magnificent job, and by the end of the war women made up about one-third of what was known as the replacement workforce, as against 45 per cent supplied by soldiers, and the rest made up from various other sources, including prisoners of war. But it required something more than a lot of extra hands to make up for the lack of imported food and to avoid the real risk of the country being starved into defeat. The essential thing was to bring land that had been left to go to waste back into production. In his memoirs, Lloyd George wrote that 'the government saw quite clearly that we should have to resort to labour saving machinery on a large scale'. A Machinery Sub-Committee was set up to supply tractor units that would do ploughing work under contract. Each unit consisted of eleven tractors with trained staff. The scheme did not always work out as well as expected, often because the ploughs that had been provided by the farmers to be pulled by the tractors were not up to the job. An alternative scheme was set up that allowed individual farmers to lease tractors very cheaply with an option to buy them at the end of the war. At first most of the tractors had to be imported from America, and over the war years some 3,000 machines were brought over.

Not all the tractors were impressively efficient. The Titan, produced by the International Harvest Company of Chicago, for example, was a cumbersome brute. It looked ungainly, with a large water tank on the front, used for cooling the two-cylinder engine. The tractor had two forward gears and one reverse, but a top speed of 3mph. Thousands were bought at £500 each. Henry Ford had been experimenting with tractor design since 1907, but the company was content with manufacturing the highly successful Model T, so he set up a new company, Henry Ford & Son Corporation, to start production. He agreed to start production in Britain in 1918, but it came a little too late to have any effect on the war effort.

One British company had made a modest start in manufacturing tractors. The Saunderson Tractor and Implement Company of Bedford was among the pioneers. H.P. Saunderson who had founded the company had demonstrated his first 'self-moving vehicle' in 1898, but in the early days he had great difficulty persuading farmers to use the machines, and output was a mere one machine per month for the first eight years. He was very much a hands-on engineer. He took personal responsibility for every aspect of the design, creating the patterns for all the individual parts. During the early years of the war, production was increased and the company was producing four different models of 10hp, 18hp, 30hp and 50hp. In 1917, the government finally got round to giving them a major order of 400 tractors with the same number of three-furrow ploughs. They were given just six months to complete the order so as to meet the emergency food shortage that was facing the nation. The ploughs had to be set to work in order to assure a bumper harvest in the summer of 1918. Without the efficiency of tractor ploughing it is doubtful if enough land could have been made available for crops: the tractor was as vital to the war effort as the tank or the aeroplane.

It was not only the farmers who were being urged to help with the emergency. Everyone was being encouraged to grow crops wherever there was spare land. In 1916 a government report was issued, praising the work of the Land Cultivation Society in London: 'The work which has been done ... has proved that excellent crops of potatoes and other vegetables can be grown on most unpromising sites, and if similar efforts are made in other urban areas a very substantial addition will be made to the food supplies of the nation.'

As well as trying to get everyone to grow more food, the authorities also mounted a campaign to make the most of what was available, through the National Food Economy League. This included trying to persuade families to eat less bread, with the slogan 'The Kitchen is the Key to Victory'. And if people did want bread then they would have to make do with a rather different basic ingredient: early in 1918, the Ministry of Food issued directions to millers to mix 20lb of potatoes to every 280lb sack of flour with the unlikely comment that 'this will effect an improvement in the Bread rather than otherwise'. The campaign was not very well received. *Punch* published a cartoon showing a portly couple in a chauffeur-driven car displaying an 'Eat Less Bread' sticker on the windscreen. The government also tried to boost the food economy campaign by publishing a recipe book *Handbook for Housewives*, costing just 1*d*, which suggested various ways of using what little was available. These appeals to patriotism failed to convince people to make any dramatic changes in their eating habits, however, and by the start of 1918 some commodities were becoming very scarce. As a result, in January the government was forced to introduce food rationing for the first time. They started with sugar, but soon extended it to meat.

Thanks to the efforts throughout the war years to increase home production of food and the various methods used to persuade people to eat less, the famine that many feared never happened. The food on the table in 1918 may not have been either as tasty or as plentiful as it had been pre-war, but at least there was enough to ensure that no one actually had to go hungry. According to official statistics, the calorie intake of the average citizen was much the same at the end of the war as it had been at the beginning. The nation was at least as fit and healthy on Armistice Day as it had been four years earlier when the country had first gone to war.

16

THE AFTERMATH

On the eleventh hour of the eleventh day of the eleventh month of 1918, the fighting stopped and the people of Britain looked forward to returning to normality, but were uncertain what that normality would be. Would it be a return to the world they had known before the war, or would some of the great changes of the past four years be retained through into peacetime? The general election of December 1918 was the first to be held under new legislation. The electorate now included all males over the age of 21, with the exception of that interestingly diverse trio – lunatics, felons and peers of the realm. Women had finally won the vote, but not equality. A woman had to be over 30, and either she or her husband had to be owners or occupiers of land rated at £5 per annum or more. Soldiers still overseas were also able to vote, and the count was delayed to allow their votes to be included. Lloyd George led the campaign, with his famous promise of a 'land fit for heroes', and the country returned the coalition to power, but with an overwhelmingly large majority from the Conservative Party. It looked as if it was a popular vote to return to pre-war conditions, but the figures for the numbers of votes cast give a rather different picture. Altogether the coalition polled 5,091,528 votes, electing 484 members of whom 338 were Conservative.

Labour polled 2,374,385 votes but only received 59 seats. Stanley Baldwin described the new members as 'hard faced men who looked as if they had done well out of the war'.¹ It seemed that the old brigade were back in charge, reinforced by a new breed of profiteers: it did not bode well. But there was clearly a great swell of opinion, not greatly represented in Parliament, that wanted a different future. The next few months were to give an indication of which way the pendulum would swing.

The main preoccupation of the first few months of the peace was to try and return the country to normality. The railway system had been tested to its limit for the past four years, with footplate crew trying to coax and cajole their wheezing locomotives to work efficiently, in the absence of regular maintenance and overhaul. For years the railway works had been largely given over to providing armaments and munitions, so at least there was the possibility that soon they would be back doing their proper job of keeping the system going. In the meantime, just as resources had been stretched in 1914 taking troops to the various camps and to the ports for embarkation, now they were to be just as busy for a time bringing them home again.

The railways were still under government control, even though they were still owned by individual companies. That meant that issues such as wages and working hours were still being settled by arbitration. The train crews and station staff who had done an incredible job under the most difficult conditions now looked for their reward. Instead in 1919 they found themselves and other railway workers faced by a proposed new wage structure, ostensibly to be introduced to provide a fairer system. In practice, it meant wages being cut for many grades. The Associated Society of Railway Engineers and Firemen (ASLEF) and the National Union of Railwaymen (NUR) called a strike. And after only a few days the government stepped in. They granted a request for an eight-hour working day without any form of consultation with the railway companies, and it was soon extended to other railway workers.

The war years had shown that having the whole system under central control had been more efficient than the old fragmented version, and there was a real hope among many railway workers that this might be retained. The Labour Party had recently written its famous Clause Four to its constitution, calling for the party 'to secure for the producers by hand and by brain the full fruits of their industry … upon the basis of common ownership'. That was not going to happen any time soon, but important changes were about to come. In the summer of 1919, government responsibility for the railways was removed from the Board of Trade to the newly formed Ministry of Transport under Sir Eric Geddes. He was an interesting character, who had attended various public schools, where it was said he had shown much more interest in playing rugby than in studying. Eventually he went to America, where he had a number of jobs, including as a brakeman on the Baltimore & Ohio Railway, and on his return from America managed to get a job running forestry railways in the Himalayas. So, unlike many politicians, he actually had practical experience of the work his ministry now controlled. While neither he nor the rest of the government were prepared to contemplate nationalising the railways, there was at least a realisation that the old system had to be changed. It was simply too complex and irrational to have a national network broken up between over 100 different companies, so it was decided to take 120 railway companies and divide them into four brand new groupings: the London Midland & Scottish (LMSR), London & North Eastern (LNER), the Great Western (GWR) and the Southern (SR). It inaugurated what some have called a golden age of railways: it was certainly the golden age of steam railways. With the great workshops back in business, a whole new generation of fast, powerful engines were produced, culminating in the LNER's *Mallard* that established a world speed record of 126mph for steam locomotives in 1938 – a record that has never been broken.

The British steam railways of the 1920s and '30s are looked back on with great affection by many, but elsewhere in Europe railway companies were turning in different directions. Italy had experimented with electrification on the main line between Milan and Varese as early as 1901, and in Germany diesel engine railcars were being developed, culminating in what to us is now the rather comically named

Flying Hamburger. There was nothing comical about the real machine, a vision of streamlined modernity, which was achieving average speeds of 77mph on its intercity run, compared with the British crack steam express the *Cheltenham Flyer*, which was only managing an average 72mph. The future of the railways did not lie in steam – but Britain, the country that had pioneered the railways, thanks to the experiments of daring engineers, was now slow to accept change.

Administration on the new rail network might have been more efficient, but the changes were not enough to secure the network for the future. There was a new threat that arose that would affect freight traffic in particular. Rates for freight on the railways had been pegged during the war years, but now they were allowed to rise quite steeply. In the past they had faced little competition, but now everything had changed. Motor transport had developed during the war, and it was estimated that some 80,000 servicemen had been trained in truck driving and maintenance. At the end of the war the government decided to sell off about 600,000 vehicles at very low prices.[2] There were plenty of ex-servicemen who decided that the best way to spend their war gratuities was to buy a truck and start running their own haulage business. Because they were working for themselves and anxious to build up a successful trade starting from scratch, they were prepared to work long hours and take low profits.

The sudden arrival of thousands of trucks, either bought by companies to move their own products or by individuals acting as general hauliers, presented a challenge to the railways, but there were still many bulk commodities, notably coal, that could still be handled better by rail. What the newcomers did offer, apart from cheap rates, was a door-to-door service that was very attractive. It hit the railways, but had a far stronger effect on the canals. By the 1920s many canals, especially those in railway ownership, were either being closed down altogether or were so neglected that traffic was deterred from using them. The official *Canal Bradshaw* for the 1920s lists many canal closures. One of the canals that was only partially closed, the Basingstoke, was the canal that had been used for training soldiers in the skills of boat handling. Although the book did not say so in actual words, it made it clear that the future for commercial traffic on that particular waterway was dim, but held out hope for an alternative use: 'The long level pound between Ash Lock and Basingstoke, through unsurpassed rural scenery, makes the canal an ideal resort for pleasure boating.'[3] It proved prophetic, for although the canal was soon to close to all commercial traffic and fall into disrepair, it was to find a new life after the Second World War, when volunteers began restoring it for holiday cruising. But for most of Britain's canals in the post-war years the future was bleak.

Road transport was beginning a boom time in the period immediately following the peace, though the road system and its laws could hardly be said to be keeping up with the changes. I still have my father's battered old *Michelin* guide from the early 1920s, which lists, among other things, information about the brand new road numbering system, the A and B roads, first introduced by the New Ministry of Transport, and instructions on what to do when meeting another vehicle – move over to the left. The limitations of vehicles and their power can be guessed at by the section listing 'The Principal Hills of Great Britain' – a slope of 1:10 was considered enough of a hazard to warrant a mention. But things were improving. British motor manufacturers were able to reclaim their factories from war work and new production techniques were introduced, adapting the assembly line processes developed in America by Ford. Morris at Oxford was soon establishing a reputation as a manufacturer of cheap but reliable cars. At the start of the 1920s they were turning out 300 vehicles per week, but by 1924 that had risen to 2,000 units, claiming over half of the UK market for cars. The same year the company introduced a sporty model, which instead of being given a name was just given the initial for Morris Garage – the first MG. It was an industry that was to grow in importance, while older industries declined.

The newcomer in the transport industry was flight. The aeroplane had developed enormously throughout the war years, and it seemed that the time had come to find a peacetime use. Less than a year after the end of the war, the British company, Aircraft Transport & Travel Ltd, had established a daily scheduled service between London and Paris. But the planes were still very basic, based on the early bombers. Their range was limited, and the accommodation primitive. For long-haul flights and comfortable, even luxurious accommodation, there was an alternative: the airship. The success of the Zeppelins had been all too ably demonstrated in their air raids over Britain, and at the end of the war German airship design was far in advance of anything the British had achieved. In peacetime, Zeppelin's again led the way in developing craft for civilian passengers. The LZ-127, later named the *Graf Zeppelin*, was designed to carry mail and up to twenty passengers. It made its maiden flight on 18 September 1928 and less than a month later it left Germany to fly to America. It made a special detour to pass over the White House, where the President's wife, Grace Coolidge, had laid on a party for her friends to see the flight. It then turned north, flew over Baltimore and Philadelphia and finally landed in New York 111 hours 44 minutes after take off.[4] The airship seemed the obvious choice for long-haul flights that were, at the time, well beyond the capabilities of any aeroplanes. For the British, the appeal was for flights that would be able to join the different parts of the Empire. This was to be a programme carried out by the government as a direct continuation of the work done during the war.

The base for airship development was the Royal Airship Factory at Cardington, where engineers were able to study the latest Zeppelins, captured during the war. Work began with an extensive testing programme carried out by the National Physical Laboratory. The original idea was that all development should be handed over to a civil aviation company, as the government blew hot and cold about the whole idea. It was, however, eventually decided to build two airships – one a government project at Cardington, the other a commercial one at Vickers. The government ship was the R101 that was finally completed in 1929. It set off on its maiden overseas voyage on 5 October 1930. It was as luxurious as the *Graf Zeppelin*, with fifty cabins, a dining room for sixty people, two promenade decks with windows and an impressive lounge. There was even a smoking room, not what you would expect to find directly under a vast bag of inflammable hydrogen, but it was lined with asbestos. The first flight was a high-prestige event and the air minister himself, Lord Thomson, was among the passengers: it was also its last. The R101 crashed in France, killing forty-eight of the fifty-four passengers and crew. It brought the whole airship development programme in Britain to a full stop. What had looked to be one of the most promising developments to come out of the war, and was all set to find a new role in peacetime, was at an end.

International air travel was very limited in the post-war years. When Britain finally began to operate a national airline, Imperial Airways, in 1924, it owned a grand total of thirteen planes. For the vast majority of people, overseas travel meant just that – going overseas in a ship. The shipbuilders who had been struggling in the final years of the war to make up for the shipping lost to the U-boats hoped for better things in peacetime. They were to be disappointed.

Before the war, British-built ships had commanded over 60 per cent of the world market, but by 1920 the share had fallen to 40 per cent, due to a number of different factors. First, there was growing competition from abroad, particularly in Scandinavia, where shipyards were looking to improve construction methods and technologies in order to reduce building costs. British yards were slow to follow. In an industry famous for periods of boom and slump, it had always seemed preferable to invest in a large force of manual workers who could be laid off when things were bad and re-employed when trade improved, rather than to have capital tied up in expensive machinery that could lie idle for long periods. Foreign orders for ships were disappearing, but there had always been a strong demand at home. As long as the red ensign reigned, the shipyards would be busy. Unfortunately, however, there was a worldwide slump in trade, which affected everyone. Suddenly there was a situation of too many ships chasing too little trade; the demand for new vessels all but disappeared. The effect could be seen in shipyards all over Britain.

John Brown's on the Clyde was one of the industry's giants, and what happened there was all too typical. At first it seemed the good times had returned. In 1914 there were around 9,000 men employed at an average wage of £1 16s 8d per week: by 1920 the workforce was much the same, 9,297 men employed – but pay had risen to £4 2s. Then the slump started. In 1921 the workforce was down to 6,322 and pay to £3 13s 5d. The following year was even worse, with man-power all but halved at 3,635 and pay was down yet again to £2 14s.[5]

With the demand for merchant shipping in catastrophic decline, the main hope was for orders for the navy. But it was universally believed that the world had just endured 'the war to end wars' and disarmament talks were the order of the day, not rearmament. An international meeting was called in Washington in November 1921 and it was agreed that all work on capital ships should be halted and there would be a ten-year ban on building warships. The industry was facing an unprecedented slump that would culminate in many shipyards closing for good. The most famous victim was Palmer's of Jarrow, in effect the town's only industry. The men of Jarrow set off to march to London in 1936, gaining huge public sympathy, but no practical help from the government to get them out of the desperate situation in which they found themselves. The industry would never regain its unique position of world leader and was to begin a period of decline that was to culminate in the virtual disappearance of all commercial merchant ship construction by the end of the century.

The shipyard industry had, like many others, employed large numbers of women during the war, but it had always been clearly understood that when peace came and the men returned home the women would have to leave to make way for them. The employment of women in what had previously been considered work that only men could – and should – do had represented one of the great social changes of the war. They had proved themselves over and over again to be able to turn their hands to almost any kind of work, and now they were expected simply to pack up and either go home to be a housewife and mother or to take one of the jobs that women had tra-ditionally done in earlier times. One of those jobs that had employed enormous numbers was domestic service.

The *London Gazette* carried out a survey of women doing war work in 1917 and found that over 70,000 of them had previously

been servants. Another survey in 1919 found that 65 per cent said
they would never be servants again and another 5 per cent said
they would go back to the work, but not on the same conditions
that they had endured before the war. This time they would want
to be paid at least £40 per year, have two and a half days off per
week and have a right to choose their own uniforms. They had
discovered the value of independence, and they were not going
to be the subservient creatures that they had been in the past. This
clearly alarmed the would-be employers, as an article in *The Times*
made clear: 'At present mistresses seeking maids have to adopt a
more democratic attitude than they would have thought possible
some years ago and pay a wage which they would have thought
ample for their own dress allowances'.⁶ The idea of a lady having
to pay a servant as much as she spent on new dresses must have
horrified many. It was apparently all down to the 'greater freedom
of the munitions factories'. Whatever the reason, by the middle
of 1919, for every one woman looking for work as a servant there
were four vacancies. The matter was considered sufficiently serious
to be raised in Parliament. It was revealed that women attending
employment exchanges were refusing to accept jobs as servants.
The Minister of Labour made it clear, to the accompaniment of
cheers, that 'it is not open to anyone to refuse work because they
do not like it' and reported that 22,000 girls had lost their unemployment pay for doing so. One member even suggested that the
situation was so grave that servants might have to be conscripted.
The results of this change of attitude were, it seemed to the better
off in the country, unimaginably dire: 'the degradation of the
middle class woman into a mere household drudge', which can be
translated as forced to do their own housework instead of paying a
lower-class woman to do it for her – or, indeed persuading her husband to lend a hand. Whatever the authorities might have thought
of doing, in the event the women were not going to return to the
drudgery of the past.

Women might not have gone back to their former roles, but nor
were they given the opportunity to follow up the skills they had

acquired during the war years. Industries that had been virtually all-male preserves in the past were to be so again. And it was not just the attitude towards women that reverted to pre-war status: industrial relations were also soon back where they had been before. The 'no strike' agreements had largely held through the war years, but soon the old fights were resumed. In 1919 it has been estimated that 2.4 million workers went on strike, and nowhere was the conflict more bitter than in the mining industry.

At the end of the war there were high hopes that better times would arrive and that attitudes would change. The industry had been under government control during the war and now the miners pushed for nationalisation to be made permanent. At the same time they asked for a 30 per cent pay rise and a six-hour working day. It is doubtful if anyone expected to get such major concessions: it was an opening position for bargaining. In the event the demands were simply refused outright and a strike was called. At this point, Lloyd George stepped in. He offered to set up a commission that would look at pay and conditions and consider the question of public ownership. It went further than earlier enquiries in that it was agreed that the miners' union would be fully represented at the talks.

Things went well at first. There was an interim settlement on pay, which went some way towards meeting the union demands, which it was agreed would be considered in full by the enquiry. The chairman Sir John Sankey listened to the arguments and reported back to the government that he thought there was a good case for public ownership. But although Lloyd George was not personally totally opposed to the idea he headed a government with a large Conservative majority. They were not going to agree to a measure that smacked of Bolshevism, and the idea of improved pay and conditions was equally unacceptable. The industry was facing a new economic problem. The Treaty of Versailles had imposed punitive measures on the defeated Germans, which may have appeased those, especially the French, who wanted revenge but made no economic sense. One of them required Germany to supply cheap coal to the victorious nations: good news for the customers, bad news for the British coal industry.

With the enquiry going nowhere, strike action was again threatened, and another interim pay award was made to last for six months. By now the government had had quite enough of the troublesome coal industry, relinquished all its powers and left it to the owners and miners to sort out for themselves. Lord Birkenhead, who had been involved in many of the talks, said of the miners: 'I should call them the stupidest men in England if I had not previously had to deal with the owners.'

The situation was now back to where it had been at the start of the century. The day that the mine owners regained control of the industry they declared they were going to cut wages and, when the unions objected, they locked out the miners. Theoretically the miners were in a Triple Alliance with the dockers and railwaymen and called on them for support, which they reluctantly gave for a short time, but soon ducked out of the fight. The miners gave their agreement a new name: 'the Cripple Alliance'. Eventually the men were forced back to work, accepting severe pay cuts that in some regions were as high as 40 per cent. The days of wartime co-operation for the general good were well and truly over and the industrial world seemed to be back to what it had been pre-war. The war of shells and bullets had given way to the old war of strikes and lockouts.

This sort of conflict did not plague every industry, but there were other ways in which a return to pre-war practices could be equally damaging. The textile industry still contained too many mills, working with antiquated machinery and old ideas, where the rest of the world was modernising. The lack of raw cotton that had held back British factories had provided an opportunity for others to grab at their markets. India had become a serious competitor. Where once the country that grew the cotton had actually been forced to import finished cloth from Lancashire, it was now not only supplying its own needs but exporting as well. Where Lancashire companies such as Platt's had been world famous as manufacturers of textile machinery, the latest and most innovative machines were now being designed and built in Switzerland. The woollen industry had been given a breath of life with the demand for uniforms, but that was over.

The cotton industry had lost markets because of the war, which they would never regain.

The First World War had seen immense changes in British industrial life. In many areas there had been great technological changes that were to be carried through to the peacetime years. The infant motor and aircraft industries were growing to maturity. In other areas, industries reverted to old practices, with a reluctance to change. Shipbuilding and textiles both entered a period of decline from which they never recovered. There were important social changes, notably the attitude towards women. They had got the vote – or at least some of them had – which the suffragettes had fought so hard for and they had started to reject many of the old attitudes. In order to meet the demands being made on all industries, the government had been forced to recognise trade unions as representatives of the workforce and involve them in decision making. They had even to do the previously unthinkable – take away the rights of industrialists to run their own concerns however they chose and insist on controlling industries for the general good. Many thought that this would be the start of a new age, where such ideas would be carried over to peacetime. It was not to be. There would be no Red Revolution in Britain.

Whatever happened to British industry in the years after the war, one thing is beyond dispute. In the four years from 1914 to 1918 it served the country well. The sacrifices made to keep the economy going and to match the technological battle with Germany may not have been as painful as those made by the 750,000 who died in the trenches, but they were very real. The efforts of working men and women should be remembered with pride, just as we remember those who fought on the battlefields of Flanders and the Middle East.

NOTES

Chapter 1

1. A.J.P. Taylor *English History 1914–1945*, 1965
2. The story of the early development of the steam carriage is told in Anthony Burton *Richard Trevithick*, 2000
3. Anthony Burton *The Rise and Fall of British Shipbuilding* (2nd edition) 2013
4. *The Times* 17 December 1914
5. *The Times* 5 June 1914
6. *The Times* 8 May 1915
7. Quoted in I.T. Greig 'The Convoy System and the Two Battles of the Atlantic' *Military History Journal* December 1984
8. *The New York Times* 8 May 1915
9. Quoted in Christopher Chant *The Zeppelin* 2000
10. *The Times* 13 September 1915
11. O.G. Barrington Jones *Dover and the War 1914–18*
12. Taylor, op. cit.

Chapter 2

1. T.C. Barker and C.I. Savage *An Economic History of Transport in Britain* 1959
2. Quoted in Frank Ferneyhough *The History of Railways in Britain* 1975
3. *The Railway Clearing House Handbook of Railway Stations* 1904
4. Quoted in Edwin A. Pratt *British Railways in the Great War* 1921. This monumental work is the fullest account of the railways in these years and much of the material for this chapter has used this book as a main source of information

5. Ibid.
6. Alfred Williams *Life in a Railway Factory* 1915
7. Ferneyhough, op. cit.
8. For a fuller account, with all the details of the signalling sequence that caused the accident, see L.T.C. Rolt *Red for Danger* (3rd edition) 1976

Chapter 3

1. *Great Eastern Railway Magazine* September 1916
2. *Dictionary of National Biography*
3. Edwin A. Pratt *British Railways and the Great War* 1921
4. Miles Clarke 'Wartime Canal Boatmen' *Journal of the Railway and Canal Historical Society* March 1996
5. Quoted in John Philips *Inland Navigation* 1805
6. *The Times* 22 January 1916

Chapter 4

1. *Daily Telegraph* 4 September 1914
2. Quoted in Midge Mackenzie *Shoulder to Shoulder* 1975
3. Pratt, op. cit.
4. Mackenzie, op. cit.
5. Quoted in Anthony Burton *The Rise and Fall of British Shipbuilding* 1994
6. *The Times* 15 September 1916
7. *The Times* 12 December 1916, Quoted in Taylor, op. cit.
8. Quoted in Taylor, op. cit.
9. Statistics from the Standing Joint Committee on Women's Industrial Organisation, quoted in Deborah Thom *Women and Work in Wartime Britain* Imperial War Museum papers

Chapter 5

1. Taylor, op. cit.
2. *The Times* 16 March 1915
3. Douglas T. Hamilton *High Explosive Shell Manufacture* 1916 contains a complete account of all aspects of manufacture as carried out in the middle of the war
4. Imperial War Museum papers 77/156/1
5. Oral history recorded at www.dartfordarchive.org.uk
6. Much of the information on this factory is taken from Chris Brader *Timbertown Girls* PhD thesis, University of Warwick
7. Rebecca West 'The Cordite Makers' *Daily Chronicle* 6 November 1916

8. *The Bombshell*, the house magazine of the Templeborough munitions factory
9. Mrs Ellis Chadwick 'A Visit to a Munitions Factory' *The World's Work* 1916
10. *The Times* 24 June 1918
11. Quoted in Hamilton, op. cit.

Chapter 6
1. *The Times* 23 April 1857
2. Letter quoted in L.T.C. Rolt *Isambard Kingdom Brunel* 1957
3. A full account of the industry by an insider is F.H. Hatch *The Iron and Steel Industry of the United Kingdom under War Conditions* 1919
4. *Workington as an Iron and Steel Producing Centre* 1908
5. J. Laing and R.T. Rolfe *A Manual of Foundry Practice* 1934
6. Quoted in Samuel Smiles (ed.) *James Nasmyth, An Autobiography* 1883

Chapter 7
1. Quoted in Joseph Wickham Roe *English and American Tool Builders* 1916
2. Ibid.
3. Quoted in Charles Singer, E.J. Holmyard, A.R. Hall and Trevor L. Williams *A History of Technology Vol. V* 1958
4. David Pam *The Royal Small Arms Factory Enfield & its Workers* 1998

Chapter 8
1. Michael and Molly Hardwick 'Entertainment' in John Canning (ed.) *1914* 1967
2. Phyllis Dare *Strand Magazine* January 1914
3. Terry Ramsaye *A Million and One Nights* 1926
4. *Manchester Guardian* 4 December 1914
5. Anthony Burton *Opening Time* 1987
6. *Hucknall Express* 21 October 1915
7. Recorded by Ernie Mayne 1917

Chapter 9
1. Rudolf Diesel in Preface to A.P. Chalkley *Diesel Engines* 1912
2. Michael E. Ware *The Making of the Motor Car* 1976
3. 'A Director' *Commercial Motor Vehicles* 1916

Chapter 10
1. For the full story of traction engine development see Anthony Burton *Traction Engines* 2000

2. Quoted in John Glanfield *The Devil's Chariots* 2001. This book contains a very full account of the early development of tanks
3. *The Times* 27 November 1925
4. Glanfield, op. cit.
5. *The Times* 27 November 1925

Chapter 11

1. Anon *Two Hundred and Fifty Years of Shipbuilding by the Scotts at Greenock* 1961
2. J. Mitchell *Shipbuilding and the Shipbuilding Industry* 1926
3. Transcripts from the Oral History Project, McLean Museum, Greenock
4. Tyne and Wear Archive Service
5. Sir Eustace H.W. Tennyson d'Eyncourt *A Shipbuilder's Yarn* 1949
6. Michael Moss and John R. Hume *Shipbuilders to the World, 125 years of Harland and Wolff* 1986
7. Bartram's Wartime Diary, Tyne and Wear Archive Services
8. Norman Longmate *Milestones in Working Class History* 1975

Chapter 12

1. Quoted in L.T.C. Rolt *The Aeronauts* 1966
2. Christopher Chant *The Zeppelin* 2000
3. Wing Commander T.R. Cave-Browne-Cave 'Some Airship Personalities' *Journal of the Royal Aeronautical Society* 1966. This issue was the centenary issue of the society, with a number of articles, several of which will be quoted as *JRAS*
4. J. Laurence Pritchard 'A Century of British Aeronautics' *JRAS*
5. A very full account of these early years can be found in Hugh Driver *The Birth of Military Aviation in Britain 1903–1914* 1997
6. *The Times* 24 January 1906
7. Peter Berresford Ellis and Piers Williams *By Jove, Biggles* 1985
8. Hessell Tiltman 'Looking Backwards' *JRAS*
9. A.J. Sutton Pritchard 'Admiralty Air Department 1915' *JRAS*
10. Quoted in Driver, op. cit.
11. Derek N. James *Gloster Aircraft Company* 1999

Chapter 13

1. The story of the sappers is told in more detail in Anthony Burton *Miners* 2013
2. Arthur Stockwin *Thirty-odd Feet below Belgium* 2005
3. George Orwell *The Road to Wigan Pier* 1937

4. H. Stanley Jevons *The Coal Trade* 1915
5. Minutes of the meeting of the War Cabinet, 27 September 1917

Chapter 14

1. Edward Baines *History of the Cotton Manufacture in Great Britain* 1835
2. This description by wool workers and others in this section are taken from tapes recorded by the Stroudwater Textile Trust
3. Colum Giles and Ian H. Goodall *Yorkshire Textile Mills* 1992
4. Katrina Honeyman *Well Suited: A History of the Leeds Clothing Industry* 2000
5. *The Times* 19 January 1917
6. Ibid. 31 July 1917
7. G.B. Gathar and S.G. Beri *Indian Economics* 1929

Chapter 15

1. David Lloyd George *Memoirs* 1934
2. Christopher M. Reason *Agriculture and Authority* 1982 thesis
3. P.E. Dewey 'Government Provision of Farm Labourers in England and Wales' *Economic History Review* 1979
4. Recruitment programme, Museum of English Rural Life (MERL) archives
5. Circular letter, 15 April 1918 (MERL)
6. Food Production Department Report, 20 August 1918 (MERL)
7. Anonymous notes (MERL)
8. Letter from the Women's Board, Food department, 5 May 1917 (MERL)

Chapter 16

1. Figures and quote from Charles Loch Mower *Britain Between the Wars* 1955
2. Statistics from Frank Ferneyhough *The History of Railways in Britain* 1975
3. Henry Rodolph de Salis *A Handbook of Inland Navigation* 1928
4. Christopher Chant *The Zeppelin* 2000
5. John Brown Company Pay Bill Book, 1914–25, Business Records Centre, Glasgow University
6. *The Times* 29 May 1919

INDEX